GET that RAISE!

Other Entrepreneur Personal Finance Pocket Guides Include:

- *Dirty Little Secrets: What the Credit Bureaus Won't Tell You*
- *Why Rent? Own Your Dream Home!*
- *Mortgages and Refinancing: Get the Best Rates*
- *Buy or Lease a Car Without Getting Taken for a Ride*

Entrepreneur MAGAZINE'S POCKET GUIDES

GET that RAISE!

Entrepreneur Press and
Jason R. Rich

EP
Entrepreneur® Press

Editorial Director: Jere L. Calmes
Advisory Editor: Jack Savage
Cover Design: Beth Hansen-Winter
Production and Composition: studio Salt
Envelope art: ©Miguel Angel Salinas Salinas
Tip art: ©Miguel Angel Salinas Salinas

Library of Congress Cataloging-in-Publication Data

Rich, Jason R.

Get that raise!/by Entrepreneur Press and Jason R. Rich.

p. cm.

ISBN-13: 978-1-59918-064-9 (alk. paper)

ISBN-10: 1-59918-064-2 (alk. paper)

1. Promotions. 2. Wages. 3. Employee fringe benefits. 4. Career development. I. Entrepreneur Press. II. Title.

HF5549.5.P7R53 2007

650.1′2—dc22 2007003707

Printed in Canada

12 11 10 09 08 07 10 9 8 7 6 5 4 3 2 1

Contents

Appendix

Acknowledgments

Thanks once again to Jere Calmes, Karen Thomas, Stephanie Singer, and Ronald Young at Entrepreneur Press for inviting me to work on this project and on the *Pocket Guides* series.

My never ending love and gratitude goes out to my closest friends—Mark, Ellen (as well as Ellen's family), Ferras, and Chris, who are all important people in my life.

I'd also like to thank my family for all of their support, and give a shout out to my Yorkshire Terrier "Rusty" (www.mypalrusty.com). Yes, he has his own web site, so please check it out!

Preface

Are you one of the many millions of workers out there who believe you're overworked, underpaid, and not appreciated by your employer? This is an all-too-common predicament to be in, especially if you're living paycheck to paycheck and have little or no job security. Unfortunately, unless you're willing to quit your job and start your own business in order to become your own boss, you'll need to continue working for someone else. The trick, however, is to discover and pursue employment opportunities that allow for upward mobility, career advancement, and the compensation you deserve.

Get That Raise! is all about how to obtain the raise or promotion you deserve based upon your education, skills, experience, occupation, employer, and choice of industry in which to work. In almost all cases, the salary you're paid is based on the perceived value you provide to your employer. Many factors, however, help to determine how much an employer is willing to pay you. By understanding these factors and their importance to your employer, you'll be in a much better negotiating position.

Doing some basic research (which you'll learn how to do by reading this book) will help you determine what you're capable of earning, based upon the following five factors:

1. The value you offer to your employer
2. Your experience, education, and skill set
3. Your geographic area
4. Your occupation, job title, and industry
5. Current market conditions

From this book, you'll learn the secrets of goal setting and how to develop a career path that will help put you on the road to success. If you want to earn more money or pursue a job with a more impressive title, it's important to understand that there is no substitute for hard work, perseverance, and the willingness to transform yourself into the type of "model employee" that is in high demand among employers everywhere. The information in this book will show you the importance of building and expanding your skill set, and how to best use your education, experience, and personality to land the highest paying jobs possible.

Like all of the books in *Entrepreneur Magazine's Personal Finance Pocket Guide* series, this one is designed to be informative

TIP

According to the U.S. Department of Labor, as of June 2005, workers in the United States earned an average of $18.62 per hour. White-collar workers earned an average of $22.96 per hour, while blue-collar workers earned an average of $15.87 per hour. Recent increases in the minimum wage, plus inflation and cost-of-living increases, have now raised these hourly rates a bit.

and easy to understand, and to quickly provide you with the knowledge you need—in this case, to earn a raise or promotion. Throughout this book, you'll see Raise Lingo You Should Know boxes that define key terms you'll need to understand. You'll also find Tip and Warning boxes that are filled with tidbits of important information. To make achieving your career-related goals and objectives easier, this book is also chock full of easy-to-use checklists and worksheets.

While it's important to understand that there are no guaranteed solutions for obtaining a raise or landing a promotion, this book will teach you how to transform yourself into the ideal candidate for earning what you truly deserve, based upon your on-the-job performance, accomplishments, education, skills, merit, and potential. Regardless of what job title you currently hold or what industry you work in, your quest to constantly improve your skill set, gain valuable new

TIP

To learn more about all of the books in the popular *Entrepreneur* Magazine's Personal Finance Pocket Guide series, visit www.entrepreneurpress.com. To learn about other books written by bestselling author Jason R. Rich, visit his web site at www.jasonrich.com.

experiences, broaden your education and knowledge base, and pursue an upwardly mobile career path is essential to your long-term success.

There's an age-old saying that "knowledge is power." Well, in this case, the knowledge you acquire from this book and through research will help you earn more money and pursue your career-related goals. In addition to this book, one of the most valuable resources at your disposal is the internet. If you're serious about obtaining a raise or promotion and advancing your career, you'll want to have access to the internet for a variety of reasons that will be outlined later. In each chapter of this book, you'll find references to career-related web sites and other online tools and resources that can be extremely valuable to job seekers or anyone interested in pursuing a raise or promotion.

Each chapter of *Get That Raise!* focuses on a different topic relating to earning a raise, pursuing a promotion, finding higher paying employment opportunities, or enhancing your overall value as an employee in today's highly competitive work force. So if you believe you deserve a raise or promotion, this book can be extremely helpful, first in analyzing your current employment and career situation, and then in improving it.

Earning a raise or promotion will require you to invest time, effort, and hard work. Unfortunately, there are no shortcuts or substitutes for this process. You can use this book, however, to help you do it faster and be more efficient and effective in your efforts. So, if you're ready to get started, turn the page and begin analyzing your current employment situation.

—Jason R. Rich
www.jasonrich.com

CHAPTER 1

Analyzing Your **Current Situation**

WHAT'S IN THIS CHAPTER

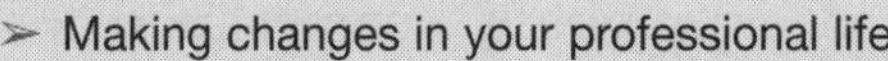

- Making changes in your professional life

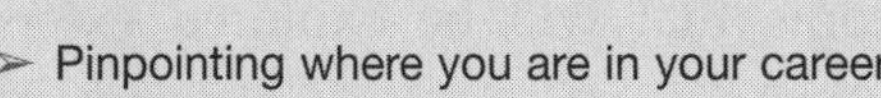

- Pinpointing where you are in your career

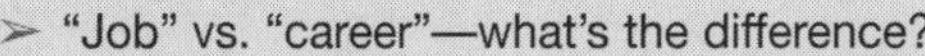

- "Job" vs. "career"—what's the difference?
- Deciding where you want your career to go
- Establishing and achieving career-related goals
- Networking your way to success
- Do you deserve a raise?

Just about everyone who holds a job believes that they should be paid more and that they're overworked, underappreciated, and not as successful as they deserve to be. Well, maybe this is true. The majority of people, however, are not earning what they truly deserve and achieving their goals because of the career-related decisions they've made thus far and their lack of willingness or know-how to change their current situation for the better.

Sure, you may want a *raise* or *promotion*. Who wouldn't? The big question is, do you deserve it? Are you valuable enough to your current employer to justify being paid more? Is your value being overlooked, or is credit for your hard work being usurped by someone else? Right now, in your current employment situation, are you being undercompensated for the work you do based on what's standard within your company, industry, and geographic area? Are you exceeding the expectations of your employer, based upon your job description, but not being properly compensated for your efforts? (This is a topic that will be explored extensively throughout this book.)

RAISE LINGO — You Should Know

Raise. When your employer decides to pay you more money for continuing to work in the same job you already possess. Your responsibilities and job title don't necessarily change, but your salary or compensation package improves. Some employers offer a raise to employees who remain on the job for a predetermined period of time. Others reward employees with raises for achieving specific milestones, accomplishments, or work-related goals. A raise is a preset amount of money that is reflected on an ongoing basis within your weekly, monthly, or annual paycheck. This is different from a one-time bonus or commission check.

Promotion. A promotion involves receiving a new job title, a new set of work-related responsibilities, a new set of expectations from your employer, and often a salary increase. A promotion can move you a step up the proverbial corporate ladder. Or it can be a "lateral promotion," which means you're given a different set of responsibilities, but the same salary and compensation package, plus you maintain your current position in the overall corporate hierarchy where you work. Typically, employers reward employees who are dedicated, provide added value, exceed expectations in terms of performance, or achieve specific milestones. Employees must typically demonstrate their competence, qualifications, willingness and ability to take on new responsibilities, and greater value to an employer before they'll be considered for a promotion.

Before you pursue obtaining a raise or promotion, which is what this book is all about, it's essential that you understand where you are now in terms of your career. More importantly, you must also develop a plan for where you want to be in 1, 3, 5, and even 10 years down the road. If you carefully define realistic *goals*, you'll give yourself an edge by having a clear path to follow—a roadmap for your career and professional life. This is what's referred to as a *career path*.

Career-related goal. A career objective you set for yourself that will somehow help you achieve more success in the future. A goal has a defined purpose, benefit, and deadline associated with it.

Career path. Your career path is your proverbial roadmap for getting from the job you have now (or plan to get) to the dream job you want in the future. Each new job or position you take on throughout your career should move you one step closer to achieving your ultimate career goal(s). Ideally, you want to demonstrate a career path that has upward mobility, allowing you to earn more money, learn new skills, gain additional experience, and take on a higher level of responsibility with each new job or position you acquire.

Determining exactly what you want to achieve will make it much easier to successfully accomplish your objectives by adopting a well-thought-out and organized plan. As you'll discover, a goal is a mission you set for yourself that has a defined purpose, benefit, and deadline. When a goal seems too big, it's essential that it be broken down into a series of smaller, more achievable goals. Each time you accomplish a minigoal, you'll be that much closer to achieving your big goal, which should be your overall objective. So when you string together a handful of career-related goals, you've got the makings of a career path that can and will lead you to success.

This chapter focuses on helping you discover where you are now from a career standpoint. It will also help you explore what you want your professional future to hold and help you set realistic goals for yourself. You will be able to determine if what you really want and deserve is a pay raise, or if a promotion is what's more important to you. Through self-analysis, you may discover that you're stuck in a dead-end job that may offer a small periodic pay raise, if you're lucky, but that over the long term will not help you achieve any of your professional goals and dreams.

Every job you take on should be a stepping stone to the next one—a job that's better. Each new job should provide you with more responsibilities and experience, teach you new skills, offer you better compensation, and ultimately help you become even more valuable as an employee. It's all about climbing the corporate ladder, whether you spend your entire career working for a single employer (something that's rare these days) or seek out a new employment opportunity every few years with a different employer that will lead to bigger and better opportunities for you.

As you'll discover, over the short term, simply earning a pay raise for the hard work you do may be the right step forward. Over the long term, however, pursuing that next promotion and somehow moving your career forward may be significantly more important to your overall well-being, financial security, and professional happiness.

Life is all about making decisions. If you exclusively rely on your employer to make career-related decisions for you and take a backseat to moving your own career forward, you can be confident that your career will move forward very slowly (if it moves forward at all). *Get That Raise!* will help you set career-related goals for yourself and teach you how to achieve them.

Making Changes in Your Professional Life

In order to bring about change in your life, career, and financial situation, you'll need to follow these six important steps:

1. Become a believer in your ability to bring about change.
2. Determine what your personal strengths are and how they can be used to help you bring about the change you desire.
3. Throw away any and all negative thoughts or fears that could hold you back from taking the steps necessary to bring about the desired change.
4. If you don't have the know-how to bring about the changes you desire, seek help from superiors, mentors, friends, family members, educators, or anyone else who might provide the support and instruction you require.
5. Be willing to take risks. Those who are willing to take professional risks often receive the biggest gains. Of course, you want to carefully think through all of your decisions and make intelligent choices about your career. Without risk, there can be no reward.
6. Find the right path to follow by focusing on your wants, needs, goals, and dreams, and then follow that path without losing your focus and dedication.

Pinpointing Where You Are in Your Career

Before you can figure out where you want to go in terms of your career, it's important to figure out where you are now and focus on your unique skill set, education, and work-related experiences that make you employable. You should also take a close look at the job you have now and determine if it's one that offers future upward mobility and the chance to move your career forward.

Filling out Figure 1.1 will help you better understand your current situation. This will help you determine what, if anything, you need to adjust in order to reach your long-term goals and ultimately improve your income.

Based on your answers in the questionnaire, you should be able to formulate a good understanding of what your current

TIP

It's essential that while you're working hard and doing everything possible to meet and exceed the expectations of your current employer in terms of your work-related responsibilities, you also focus on your own professional goals and take the steps necessary to achieve them. Nobody is going to do this for you. It's easy to make excuses and place blame on your employer for paying you too little, working you too hard, or having overzealous expectations of you. If, however, you don't like where you are now in your career and think you deserve more, it's entirely your responsibility to bring about changes in your professional life. Seek out opportunities—don't just sit around and wait for things to happen.

FIGURE 1.1: CURRENT JOB/CAREER ASSESSMENT QUESTIONNAIRE

Answer each of the following questions as honestly as possible, using as much detail as you can in order to help you gain a complete perspective on your current employment situation. Skip any questions that are not applicable.

What job title do you hold now? ______________________________

According to the company's job description, what are your primary responsibilities? ______________________________

____

____

Based on your actual experience, what are your primary job responsibilities? ______________________________

____

How long have you had this job? ______________________________

How long have you been working for your employer? ____________

What is your current weekly/monthly salary? ________________

What is your take-home pay (after taxes and other deductions)?

____

How much more would you like to be earning? ______________

How much more do you believe you deserve to be earning? _______

If you believe you are being underpaid, what research have you done to support this? ______________________________

____

____

FIGURE 1.1: CURRENT JOB/CAREER ASSESSMENT QUESTIONNAIRE, CONT.

If you were earning more money, how would your quality of life improve? What would you use the extra income for? ___________

____

____

What benefits or perks do you receive (such as health insurance, employee discounts, paid vacation time, and child care)? ________

____

____

What job-related benefits or perks are the most important to you?

____

____

What job-related benefits or perks would you like that you don't receive?

____

____

What work-related skills do you possess that allow you to meet the responsibilities of your job?___________

____

____

Do you possess any work-related skills that are not being fully used in your position? If so, what are they? ___________

____

____

FIGURE 1.1: CURRENT JOB/CAREER ASSESSMENT QUESTIONNAIRE, CONT.

Are you motivated to wake up and show up for work every day? If not, what's keeping you from enjoying your job? ________________

____

____

What do you like best about your job? ____________________

____

____

What do you like least about your job? ___________________

____

____

Since you began working in your position, what have been your top five accomplishments or achievements? How have they benefited your employer?

1. ____
2. ____
3. ____
4. ____
5. ____

From your employer's perspective, what makes you a valuable employee? ______________________________________

____

____

FIGURE 1.1: CURRENT JOB/CAREER ASSESSMENT QUESTIONNAIRE, CONT.

From your perspective, what do you offer to your employer that makes you a valuable employee? (In addition to your skills, focus on your attitude, dedication, abilities, and untapped potential.) ______

____

____

What qualities or traits do you possess that are appealing to your employer and that set you apart from other employees? _________

____

____

Is there anything holding you back from achieving your full potential on the job and using all your skills, knowledge, education, and experience? If so, what?______________________________

____

____

If you could change one thing about your job, what would it be and why?

____

____

____

Have you recently had an employee evaluation or performance review done by your employer? If so, what was the outcome?_____

____

____

FIGURE 1.1: CURRENT JOB/CAREER ASSESSMENT QUESTIONNAIRE, CONT.

How often do employee evaluations take place where you work?

____

Does your employer offer pay raises or promote from within? If so, according to your employer, what would be required of you in order to be considered for a raise or promotion? ____________________

____

____

When would you be eligible for a raise or promotion?____________

What skills, experience, or education do you lack that could be holding you back from earning a raise or promotion?_______________

____

____

Based on what other people with your skills, education, and experience are earning, either within your company or in your industry (and within your geographic area), do you believe your salary is fair or are you being underpaid?_____________________________________

____

____

Are there other job/employment opportunities potentially available to you (perhaps with another employer) that would command a higher salary, better benefits, or a more desirable overall compensation package? If so, what would pursuing better job opportunities entail?

FIGURE 1.1: CURRENT JOB/CAREER ASSESSMENT QUESTIONNAIRE, CONT.

What would be the short- and long-term benefits for you? ________

____

____

____

What on-the-job training or education is available to you that you're not taking full advantage of? Why not? ____________________

____

____

____

employment situation is, and then use this information to help you plan a better professional future. Ultimately, you'll be happiest and the most motivated to do your job well if you're working in a job that you're truly passionate about and that you believe you're being compensated fairly to do.

"Job" vs. "Career"—What's the Difference?

A *job* offers you employment and a paycheck, but little or no career-advancement potential. A job can offer gainful employment, but have little or nothing to do with what you're interested in pursuing over the long term, or educated or trained to do from a professional standpoint.

Job. A job is something you do to earn a paycheck that involves working part time or full time for an employer. In terms of this book, a job can be a stepping stone along a career path that you define for yourself, or it can be a way to pay your living expenses and bills that doesn't necessarily have anything to do with what you were trained to do or what you'd ultimately like to do for a life-long career.

People who are desperate for a paycheck often take the first job that's offered to them, without focusing on how that job will impact their future or how it could be used as a stepping stone for advancement. For example, someone might graduate from college with a degree in advertising, but wind up working as a cashier at a retail store or in another job they have little or no interest in, simply to earn a paycheck in order to cover living expenses and pay the bills.

A career involves a long-term plan for advancement. It allows you to accept a job, but also have a goal in place to be promoted or to gain enough experience to qualify for another, more advanced and higher paying job in the same or a related field.

Pursuing a career requires a long-term goal. You'll start in one position, but have a plan, the motivation, the dedication, and the work ethic to earn a significantly better (but related) job in the future. For example, you might take an entry-level job at a company that does business in your area of expertise, but have a goal and a plan in place to become senior vice president within the next ten years. Achieving this goal will require you to periodically be promoted and to constantly work to move your career forward as you make your way up the corporate ladder. Each job will allow you to build your skill set and work-related experience, but keep you in the same field or industry.

With each new job or position you take on, you'll receive a raise and promotion, be able to improve your overall quality of life, and be one step closer to achieving your long-term career objective. Developing a career path takes planning, dedication, and the ability to always be on the lookout for new and rewarding opportunities. When an opportunity comes your way, you'll need to possess the confidence and mind-set to pursue it. Being able to successfully follow a career path, especially in today's cut-throat business world, also requires that you constantly prove yourself to your employer and become a valuable asset to that company.

The jobs offered by most employers require qualified individuals to meet a series of well-defined responsibilities. These days, few employers offer true long-term career opportunities or job security. These are things you'll need to develop for yourself by seeking out jobs or positions that offer a future, upward mobility, and potential advancement.

Dead-end job. This is a job or position that offers no possibility for advancement. The employer will not be willing to offer you a raise or promotion, regardless of your on-the-job performance, merit, or seniority with the company. The responsibilities you're given on the first day on the job will remain the same throughout your entire time holding that job or position. For most people, this is not the type of opportunity to pursue, because it really isn't an opportunity at all—it's simply a way to earn a paycheck. Most people who hold dead-end jobs wind up becoming frustrated or even hating their work.

Deciding Where You Want Your Career to Go

It's one thing to dream about becoming a top-level corporate executive, who drives a flashy sports car, is a member of a prestigious country club, and owns multiple homes. It's another thing to develop a career plan that will eventually allow those dreams to become a reality. Nobody is going to pave the way for you to achieve success. That's a responsibility you'll want and need to take on for yourself.

Once you decide what you want your professional future to hold, it becomes necessary to carefully evaluate where you are today, then figure out exactly what it will take for you to achieve your goals. This will most likely require you to develop a long-term, multistep plan that's comprised of a series of shorter-term objectives.

For example, if your goal is to become a senior vice president at your company, but now you're in an entry-level position, you need to figure out how many steps up the corporate ladder you need to climb. Each step will most likely require you to acquire additional education and training. It will also require a lot of hard work, dedication, and focus. If you determine that getting from where you are now to where you want to be will require you to earn at least five separate promotions,

☆ ☆ WARNING ☆ ☆

One of the worst mistakes you can make is to accept a *dead-end job*, which is one that offers no upward mobility or advancement opportunities. The dead-end job you're hired to fill today will come with the same responsibilities that you'll possess for as long as you're employed by that company. No new training will be offered. You will have no opportunity to develop new skills. Plus, once you've learned that job, you won't be challenged in any way. Every day, month after month, and year after year, will be exactly the same. There will be no opportunity whatsoever to earn a promotion. With the exception of an occasional cost-of-living pay increase (to keep pace with inflation), you will have no chance to dramatically increase your income. People who fall into this type of work tend to become miserable relatively quickly and experience a high level of job dissatisfaction. Whether you have an advanced degree or nothing more than a high school diploma or GED, it's essential that you avoid landing in a dead-end job. If you find yourself in this type of job, take steps to find alternate employment that will make better use of your skills, experience, education, personality, and talent, and offer you potential for advancement.

and that each promotion will be achievable after two years at that job, you will have a ten-year plan for success. This will, of course, vary greatly based on the hierarchy within your company, how and when promotions are offered, your qualifications, and various other factors.

Along the way, however, with each new promotion, you'll receive a higher salary, and better benefits, plus gain new skills that will allow you to increase your value. You should always be looking for new and exciting opportunities with other employers.

Adopting a Realistic Attitude

When setting your long-term goals, it's important that you make them achievable and realistic. If you don't have a college education and have no plans to pursue one, your chances of being promoted to an executive-level position within a Fortune 500 company are relatively slim. Likewise, if you've graduated from college after majoring in business finance, but your true interest lies in corporate advertising and marketing, you'll need to obtain additional education, experience, and training before pursuing that alternative career path.

Another unrealistic goal would be to expect to be promoted from an entry-level position to a managerial or executive-level position within a very short time, without having to prove yourself along the way. When setting goals for yourself, it's important that they be realistic. Otherwise, you'll be setting yourself up for failure and disappointment. Of course, achieving a long-term goal can represent a huge

☆ ☆ WARNING ☆ ☆

Having the right skills and overall qualifications for each position you apply for is essential. Employers will not hire you for a job you are not qualified to fill, regardless of how charming you are or how professional your attitude is. Through simple research, you can determine exactly what qualifications an employer is looking for, and then decide whether you have the ability to meet the requirements of the job (based on your education, skills, and experience).

challenge, but this becomes realistic if you have a proper long-term strategy in place.

Just as having realistic expectations is important when you are seeking out career opportunities and specific jobs, you should understand that employers will only pay you what you're worth and not a penny more. So, if you're a recent college graduate, don't expect to be hired at your dream company and be offered an executive-level salary and compensation package right at the start. This is something you'll most likely have to work toward (it is often referred to as "paying your dues").

Qualifications. Your unique combination of education, knowledge, work-related experience, skills, personality, mind-set, merit, and potential that makes you a suitable applicant to fill a specific job or position. Your qualifications will allow you to handle the requirements of a job, as well as meet or exceed an employer's expectations.

Establishing and Achieving Career-Related Goals

A goal is something you want to achieve, either in the short term or over the long term. It's also something you're willing to take action on in order to make it a reality. Goals require action—not a passive approach. For the purposes of this book, a short-term goal is anything that can be achieved within a few months, while a long-term goal is something that will most likely take a year or more to accomplish.

Goals can be set for many different reasons and fall into one of several categories. For example, you might create a series of personal goals, professional goals, and financial goals for yourself. In some cases, a professional and a financial goal, or a personal and a financial goal, may be interrelated.

A goal should have the following five ingredients:

1. A purpose
2. A defined benefit for you once it's accomplished
3. A detailed plan for achieving it
4. A deadline for achieving it
5. A course of action that you are willing and able to adopt

The difference between a goal and a dream is that a goal has these five main ingredients, while a dream is something you just think about, but never take action to achieve. Everyone has dreams. It's your responsibility to transform those dreams into achievable goals.

Goals can be monumental and life-changing in scope, or very simple. At any given time, you could easily find yourself juggling multiple personal, professional, and financial goals, which might be interrelated or totally separate. Chances are, if you look back at your life thus far, you've inadvertently set goals for yourself without realizing it. If those goals weren't achieved, it could have been because you didn't have a proper plan in place. Your plans should always be written out and referred to often.

One of the most common reasons why people don't accomplish their goals is that they abandon them midway through trying to achieve them. Life is full of distractions and setbacks. These are to be expected. Part of having a plan in place for achieving your goals is to figure out, in advance,

TIP

As you're working toward achieving your goals, one excellent strategy is to keep a written diary of your progress each day, week, or month. This will allow you to see how far along you are and better determine what still needs to be done in order to accomplish each goal. Being able to track your accomplishments and reach specific milestones you set for yourself will help to keep you motivated and focused on your overall objectives.

TIP

Consider dividing goals that seem too difficult to achieve as is into a series of smaller, more achievable, but related goals—each with its own plan and deadline. As you accomplish each minigoal, you will be one step closer to achieving your overall goal.

how you'll successfully deal with these setbacks as they arise, so they don't totally halt your progress.

It's important to understand that some of what happens in your life is out of your control. When things don't go as planned, or you suddenly find yourself faced with an entirely new set of challenges, you may be forced to revisit your list of goals and modify them. Every three to six months, review your list of long-term goals and make whatever modifications are necessary to your plan for achieving them, based on your current life situation and the progress you've already made. Having to modify your goals is common. Aborting your goals before they're achieved, however, is something you obviously want to avoid.

This book focuses primarily on your financial and professional goals. When you set a goal that involves earning a raise, that increase in income is a financial matter. When you seek a promotion, it constitutes a professional goal, as well as a financial one. After all, with a promotion will probably come a salary increase, which in turn could improve your overall quality of life. Depending on what your goals are, achieving them could impact several or all aspects of your life—in what you hope will be a very positive way.

For example, if you earn a promotion, your professional situation will change. It should move your career forward. At the same time, you'll be earning more money, which will impact your overall finances. Having more money should also allow you to improve your personal life by enhancing your standard of living or allowing you to afford nicer things. So as you consider your goals and how achieving them will benefit you (step two in the goal setting process), always think about the big picture. How will the goal benefit your personal life,

TIP

As you're defining your goals, try to anticipate what could go wrong, what obstacles you'll encounter, and what challenges you may face. At the same time, figure out how you'll deal with these situations if and when they arise. Having a plan in place before bad things actually happen will help you deal with the potential setbacks much faster and more efficiently, and with much less stress involved. Part of step three in your goal planning process should involve creating acceptable contingency plans and taking "what if" scenarios into account.

professional life, and financial life? How will it impact your overall quality of life and the lives of those around you? Also think about what the impact will be on your employer.

You've purchased this book in hopes of earning a raise or promotion, right? As you already know, this constitutes a professional and financial goal, so be sure to define that goal as specifically as possible and incorporate it into a goal setting worksheet.

Invest a few minutes now and make a detailed list of your goals. For each goal, follow the first four steps in the goal setting process, and start thinking about what you can do, beginning today, to make each goal a reality. Then, once you have your goal list completed, start implementing step five, which is to take action to start achieving each goal.

Once you complete your worksheet, refer to it often. Use separate paper or even a notebook if necessary to list all of

TIP

As you focus on creating a plan for each of your goals, consider what skills, knowledge, or experience you're lacking and what you'll need to do in order to remedy the situation and ultimately achieve the goal. The steps involved in overcoming things you lack might need to become a series of subgoals.

your goals and keep track of your progress as you work toward achieving them.

> ☆ ☆ **WARNING** ☆ ☆
>
> Never allow anyone to put down your goals or keep you from achieving them. The goals you set for yourself are very personal and should be based on what you want and what you believe you can achieve. Don't allow someone else's lack of support or pessimistic attitude to keep you from doing what's necessary to achieve the realistic goals you set for yourself.

Networking Your Way to Success

One excellent skill to develop throughout your career is your ability to network. It involves meeting new people and building long-lasting professional relationships that you can use as they're needed throughout your career. Having a large network of business acquaintances at your disposal exposes you to people with vastly different backgrounds, skills, knowledge, expertise, and experiences. Your network can provide a source of new business, referrals to other people, leads to better jobs, people to go to when you need answers, and a wide range of other opportunities. These people can help you and motivate you throughout your career.

Maintaining a network and constantly growing it is simple, but it takes a bit of creativity and a conscious effort on your

TIP

In the business world, whom you know is as important as what you know. Throughout your career, work toward building up a network of contacts and discover all of the ways you can best use these contacts to help you achieve your career-related goals and enrich your personal and professional life.

part. Always be open to meeting new people, wherever you happen to be. Learn how to become a social person who can strike up conversations with strangers. Exchange business cards whenever possible and then keep the information from those cards organized in a file, using contact management software, or in a database stored within your personal digital assistant (PDA). Keep in touch with the people in your network.

If you're searching for a new job, for example, you'll find that most of the best job openings available at companies are never advertised online or in the "help wanted" ads. Jobs are often filled through word-of-mouth. If you can use one of your contacts to make a personal introduction for you into the company you want to work for, your chances of being invited in for an interview will increase dramatically. Employers tend to favor job applicant referrals from current employees or other people they trust and do business with.

The concept behind networking is relatively simple. It's about making friends and then using those friends to help you get ahead in the business world. Of course, this goes both ways. You'll be expected to help people in your network who call upon you for favors, advice, or assistance.

If, for example, you have ten contacts in your network, keep in mind that each one of those people most likely has at least ten other people in their network. This potentially gives you access to a much broader group of people through introductions and referrals. So if you need to hire a lawyer, for example, chances are someone in your network will know a top-notch lawyer and will be willing to make an introduction on your behalf. A referral from someone you know is a lot more trustworthy than finding a potential lawyer in the Yellow Pages, for example.

Your network might include include the following:

- Anyone you come into contact with in your personal or professional life
- Current and former customers or clients
- Former classmates
- Former teachers and professors
- Friends
- Members of a professional association you belong to
- People who belong to your country club, golf club, yacht club, or health club
- People you do business with in your personal life (your doctor, lawyer, accountant, barber/hairstylist, religious leader, banker, dog groomer, personal trainer)
- People you meet online who share similar personal or professional interests

- People you meet while traveling (for business or when on vacation), such as the person sitting next to you on a train or an airplane
- Present and past co-workers
- Professional colleagues you've met at conventions and trade shows
- Relatives

If used correctly, your network can help you move ahead in the business world in many different ways. It's important, however, that you never abuse the assistance people in your network are willing to offer. Most people are more apt to help you if they believe there's some benefit in it for them, either immediately or sometime in the future.

One person in your network you might want to have help you make important career-related decisions or choose a career path is the career guidance counselor at your high school or college. These people are trained to help others define their career-related goals and fine-tune their professional interests.

Do You Deserve a Raise?

In the next chapter you'll learn the difference between wanting a pay raise and actually deserving one. If you determine you deserve a raise, Chapter 3 will teach you the best strategies for getting it. These include how to negotiate with your employer.

CHAPTER 2

Do You **Deserve a Raise?**

WHAT'S IN THIS CHAPTER

- How employers set salaries
- Determining what you should be paid
- Assessing your skills and responsibilities
- Are you entitled to a raise?
- Alternatives to earning a raise
- When to seek alternate employment
- How to ask for a raise

Before you decide to do what's necessary in order to request a raise from your employer (which will be covered in Chapter 3), you should determine whether you actually deserve a raise, as opposed to just wanting one. Most employers don't care about your personal wants (or needs for that matter). What a typical employer does care about is their own bottom line. If you've proven yourself and provided enough value to your employer, and have untapped potential that the employer can recognize, you're more apt to have your request for a raise approved. Being able to showcase recent successes and accomplishments while on the job will give credibility to your request.

As you learned in the previous chapter, a pay raise means you will earn more money for doing the same job you already have. Instead of asking for an increase in pay, however, you may find it easier to negotiate with your employer to receive additional benefits and perks, such as more paid vacation days or periodic bonuses for achieving specific objectives. Alternatives to receiving a pay raise are described later in this chapter.

Just about everyone wants to earn more money for the work they're already doing. Before you're granted a raise by your employer, however, you'll need to convince your superiors that you deserve what you're requesting. This chapter, as well as the next, will help you formulate credible negotiation strategies for obtaining the raise you want and believe you deserve.

How Employers Set Salaries

Before you start researching what someone with your overall qualifications—your education, skill set, work-related

TIP

Salaries tend to be regionally based. A midlevel manager working in New York City will typically be paid a higher salary than someone with the same job title and responsibilities who works in a smaller city, somewhere in the midwest, for example.

experience, on-the-job responsibilities, merit, and job title—should be getting paid, let's take a look at the criteria virtually all employers use to set the salaries paid to employees.

Regardless of what industry you work in or what company you work for, chances are you're paid a salary based on what your employer believes you are worth, which is in part determined by current market conditions. First and foremost, a company is concerned about its bottom line and being profitable. To achieve this, it's typically going to pay its employees as little as possible, yet have high and ever-increasing expectations of it employees.

Typically, an employer will set the salaries it pays based on the following criteria:

- The job title and description, plus the responsibilities of the position
- The overall value a specific employee offers to the employer
- The skills, experience, attitude, and education of an employee

- The employee's proven successes and accomplishments, plus on-the-job performance
- The supply and demand of labor (a qualified work force)
- Seniority of the employee
- The geographic area
- The state of the economy and financial strength of the employer
- The ability of the employee to negotiate the best compensation package possible
- What is required by state law (in terms of minimum wage), local unions, or other mandates
- What the employer's competition pays its employees

Minimum wage. The federal government has set a minimum hourly wage that employers must pay nonexempt employees. Many states have set a minimum wage that's higher than what the federal government mandates. As of 2006, the federal minimum wage for covered, nonexempt employees was $5.15 per hour. At the time this book was written, legislation was in the works to increase the federal minimum wage to $7.25 starting sometime in 2007. In Massachusetts, for example, as of January 1, 2007, the minimum wage was $7.50 per hour. Effective January 1, 2008, the Massachusetts minimum wage will increase to $8.00 per hour. Across the country, the minimum wage for jobs that involve receiving tips is significantly lower. For a listing of each state's minimum wage, visit http://en.wikipedia.org/wiki/List_of_U.S._state_minimum_wages. If your income includes receiving tips, the state minimum wages are listed at www.dol.gov/esa/programs/whd/state/tipped.htm.

Now that you understand what employers consider when setting salaries, you can begin doing your own research to figure out what you should be getting paid and also determine if your current salary is fair, based on what other people with your qualifications are being paid in your geographic area.

Determining What You Should Be Paid

How much should your employer be paying you? What's fair? The easiest way to answer this question is *not* to assume that your employer is a cheapskate and underpaying you.

☆ ☆ **WARNING** ☆ ☆

Salaries are usually *not* set by an employer based on the popularity of an employee or an employee's financial needs. Telling your employer, "I need a raise in order to make the mortgage payments on my new home, and to make the monthly car payments on my new car," is not a valid reason for asking for a raise or promotion, nor will it typically result in you receiving one. You will receive a raise if, and only if, the employer believes you provide enough value to justify the pay increase. The questions the employer will always ask are: Is this person worth more than what we're paying him right now? If we don't offer a raise, are we willing to risk her leaving the company to pursue more lucrative opportunities?

TIP

An employer is more apt to give you a raise or promotion if you can justify your request by providing your company with more value as an employee. Employers look for employees who are hardworking, dedicated, ambitious, and trustworthy, and who possess a good attitude, follow directions, and exceed (not just meet) the expectations of the employer when it comes to the responsibilities of the job they're hired to fill.

Instead, you'll need to do research to determine what the average salary is for someone with your overall qualifications. Keep in mind that while some employers have a predefined financial formula for setting salaries, there is no universal standard. In addition, every employer understands that no two people have identical qualifications. Everyone's experiences and skill sets are different—even if they've had identical training and a similar work history.

When it comes to salary research, the easiest thing you can do is take an informal survey of your co-workers to determine what they're getting paid. The problem you may run into, however, is that many people are hesitant to discuss their salaries, and most companies are extremely tight lipped about what they pay various people. While age, sex, or religious discrimination in terms of salary is technically a thing of the past, in some situations and with some employers it continues to exist, at least on some level.

If you're unable to get an accurate representation of what your co-workers are being paid, the next best thing to do is salary related research. There are a variety of resources available that will allow you to research average salary information for virtually any job title or position in any industry. Based on this research, you can then compare the salary you're earning and determine if it falls within company, industry, and geographic averages.

When doing salary related research, make sure the resources you use and the data you obtain are timely and—if possible—regionalized. Otherwise, you'll be using salary information that's based on national averages. This is fine, except that people in major U.S. cities tend to receive higher salaries than people in smaller cities or rural areas. The good news about this, however, is that the cost of living in smaller cities tends to be much lower, so in theory it all evens out.

TIP

Are you considering a move to another city to pursue a new job? Use an online cost-of-living calculator to compare how much it costs to live in one city vs. another.

There are several reasons why you should conduct your own salary research at various times in your career, including

- To determine if your current salary is fair, or if you're being underpaid;
- To figure out what you could be making if you were to switch jobs and employers;
- To evaluate a job offer from a potential employer;
- To see how moving to another city, but still pursuing the same line of work, could impact your standard of living; and
- To help determine if you deserve a raise, based on current market or industry conditions.

Resources for Conducting Salary Research

The trick to doing salary research is to figure out what people with qualifications similar to yours are currently earning both locally and nationally. This research can be done using a variety of different resources, including:

- **America's Career InfoNet** (www.acinet.org). This is an excellent resource for learning about thousands of careers and jobs. The site's "occupational profiles" include wages; employment trends; knowledge, skills, and abilities (KSAs); education and training; and web resources. National, state, and local information is available, as well as trend and wage comparisons across occupations and geographical areas. Using an online tool, you can compare wages based on job title among companies and industries locally, or see how wages compare between similar job titles and occupations across multiple states or regions. Using this tool, you can quickly determine that in 2006, for example, a "fashion designer" earned about $60,100 per year, based on a national average. But when you compare earnings for the same position in Boston, Los Angeles, and New York City, you will discover that the median salary for this job is $61,700, $52,200, and $68,000 respectively. Using another tool on this site, you can obtain an up-to-date list of the highest paying jobs, based on the level of experience and qualifications required to fill them.

- **CollegeGrad.com** (www.collegegrad.com/salaries/index.shtml). From this free web site, you can access a salary calculator (which can help you learn about base salaries associated with thousands of different positions), make use of a cost-of-living calculator, and get detailed information about more than 350 different careers (including salary data). The site also offers useful articles on topics that include salary negotiation, resume preparation, and how to prepare for job interviews.
- **Contact industry trade associations.** These groups are typically an excellent source for obtaining current and accurate salary information for jobs within the particular industries the associations cater to. You can track down professional associations that cater to your particular field of interest using the Encyclopedia of Associations (http://library.dialog.com/bluesheets/html/bl0114.html),

which is a comprehensive source of information about more than 135,000 nonprofit membership organizations worldwide.

- **JobStar Central Salary Surveys** (http://jobstar.org/tools/salary/sal-surv.php). This free web site offers salary overviews for jobs in more than 300 different industries, plus a variety of different cost-of-living calculator tools and other resources. For specific industries, the web site also provides links to other sources of salary and compensation-related data.
- **PayScale.com** (www.payscale.com / 888-219-0328). This web site offers a variety of free and fee-based services for researching salary information based on your current or desired job title and zip code. To use the free online tool, you'll need to answer a questionnaire. Based on your responses, you'll be offered an on-screen "Basic Salary Report," or you'll have the ability to purchase a comprehensive (printable) "Premium Salary Report" for about $20.
- **Salary.com** (www.salary.com / 866-275-2791). As one of the most trusted and comprehensive sources for timely and accurate salary information on the internet, this web site gives currently employed people and job seekers free access to national average salary information for thousands of job titles and occupations using the "Salary Wizard." For a one-time fee, a more personalized and highly detailed, 12- to 14-page salary report is available that's based on your specific background,

education, experience, and city. The salary and compensation experts update the data on this site monthly, based on survey responses from more than 16,000 employers.

- **U.S. Department of Labor's *Occupational Outlook Handbook.*** This resource is published in traditional book form (and available from bookstores, libraries, and the career guidance office at most high schools and colleges). The directory, which is about the size of a major city's telephone book, describes thousands of occupations and offers average salary ranges, the training and education required, the expected job prospects for several years to come, and the average working conditions for each job. You can search the directory by industry, job category, or job title. It's updated every two years. The online edition of the *Occupational Outlook Handbook* can be accessed for free at www.bls.gov/oco/. The salary information within this guide is based on national (average) data.
- **Yahoo! HotJobs Salary Calculator** (http://hotjobs.yahoo.com/salary). In addition to offering career-related articles, thousands of online "help wanted" ads, and a variety of other career-related tools (all of which are free of charge), the Salary Calculator allows you to research salary information for thousands of different job titles. National average salary data is available free of charge. Premium salary reports, which offer regional and more personalized information, are available for a fee. A premium

report requires that you complete an online questionnaire that takes about five minutes. The result is an easy-to-understand, 14-page, printable report that contains detailed information about your earning potential in your geographic area. (Premium reports are prepared by Salary.com.)

Assessing Your Skills and Responsibilities

As you learned earlier in this chapter, many different criteria are used by employers to set fair and competitive salaries for employees. One wildcard, so to speak, is your personal skill set. Because everyone's skill set is unique, this allows you to set yourself apart from other employees (or job applicants) and potentially offer greater value to an employer. By properly marketing your unique skill set to an employer, you're more apt to be offered a higher salary, especially if your skills relate directly to your ability to perform your primary job functions.

TIP

Information that is similar to that found in the *Occupational Outlook Handbook,* but is based on state-specific data, can also be found online. To access information related to your state, visit www.bls.gov/oco/oco20024.htm or www.projectionscentral.com/stprojections.asp.

Take a few minutes and compile a detailed list of all of your most useful and marketable career-related skills, then focus on which skills you believe an employer will find the most valuable. Consider the skills you've used in the past (in previous jobs), as well as skills you've acquired through your education, training, and work experience.

Any skill that allows you to better meet the responsibilities of your job, perform at peak efficiency, and meet or exceed the expectations of an employer is a skill that's worth adding to your list and showcasing to your current or potential employer at the appropriate time.

Marketable skills might include being bilingual, the capability to type 60+ words per minute, sales and telemarketing skills, proficiency using specialized computer software, the ability to train and manage others, and public speaking. No matter what type of work you do, you should be able to compile a list of at least 10 to 20 skills that make you a valuable employee or desirable applicant. Using a separate sheet of paper, make a list of your skills. Once your list is completed, refer back to it when it comes time to negotiate a pay raise or promotion, or when you seek alternate employment opportunities.

Being able to quickly identify your greatest work-related skills and demonstrate them to an employer or potential employer, and provide specific examples of how you've successfully used those skills, will be beneficial at the following times:

- When participating in an employee evaluation or performance review

- When requesting a raise
- When applying for a promotion
- When updating your resume and writing cover letters
- When applying for a new job and participating in interviews
- When deciding whether or not to pursue additional education or on-the-job training, and pinpointing what additional knowledge and experience would be beneficial to you

TIP

For help creating your list of skills, review a handful of "help wanted" ads or job descriptions to see what employers are looking for. Match up the most desired skills with those you already possess.

TIP

As you list each of your skills, think about how you've used it in the past and what the outcome was. You'll want to provide your employer (or future employer) with details about what skills you possess, how you've use them in the past, and how they can be beneficial to you and your employer in the future.

Are You Entitled to a Raise?

Once you've done research to determine what people with qualifications that are similar to yours are being paid within your company and at other companies within your geographic area, and what the average median salary is across the country, you can determine whether you are being underpaid for the work you're currently doing.

While being underpaid is one reason to be entitled to a raise, another reason would be if you're able to provide added value to your employer that goes above and beyond what you were originally hired to do. If you can demonstrate a pattern of taking on responsibilities outside of your job description and can document specific examples of successes or achievements, your employer may see the benefit of giving you a raise, especially if you've become irreplaceable or extremely valuable and the employer runs the risk of you quitting.

In the next chapter, you'll learn how to request a raise. Before doing so, however, it's essential that you truly believe it's something that you deserve and have earned. It should not be something that you just want.

Keep in mind that some employers have a predefined compensation package for every position or job title within the organization, and that there's little or no leeway or discretion when it comes to setting a specific employee's salary. For example, every sales associate within a company might earn $8.50 per hour, regardless of their qualifications or seniority. Instead of giving raises to certain people who excel at their jobs, however, the company might promote qualified candidates to the position of senior sales associate, which would come with a salary of $10 per hour and offer better perks and benefits. This would be considered a promotion, not just a raise.

Even after you decide that you deserve a raise based on your current circumstances, it will be necessary to determine whether this is a viable option based on how your employer operates. If you know your company has a policy against giving out raises, then you'll need to find an alternative way to increase your income (by earning a promotion, for example), or perhaps negotiate better perks and benefits as opposed to a higher *base salary*. If these two options aren't possible, but you're significantly more valuable to your employer than what you're being compensated for, it might be time to begin pursuing a new job with another employer who will better appreciate your qualifications and properly reward you for your work and achievements.

Base salary. This is the annual salary your employer pays you, before deductions are taken out and before any commissions, bonuses, or incentives are added.

Before asking for a raise, carefully review your job description or the employee handbook provided by your employer. If you've simply met the responsibilities of your job, you may have a tough time getting a raise approved. After all, you're simply doing what's expected of you. If, however, you've consistently exceeded your job responsibilities and the expectations of your employer (and can document how and why you've done this, along with your successes and achievements), your chances of getting the raise you deserve are much greater.

While your goal is to focus on all of your positive qualities and attributes as an employee, you can bet that your employer will consider any and all of the negatives as well. Some of the things that *will not* help you get a raise include

- regularly showing up late for work;
- not adhering to the company's dress code;
- taking longer than allowed lunch or coffee breaks;
- not meeting the responsibilities of your job;
- maintaining a poor attitude;
- not taking directions from superiors;
- not getting along with co-workers;
- missing important deadlines;
- not attending mandatory meetings;
- not following company policies or procedures;
- stealing or misusing company supplies and equipment;
- spending too much time surfing the internet for personal reasons while on the job;
- spending too much time making or accepting personal phone calls while on the job;
- not handling yourself in a professional manner around customers or clients; and
- being consistently unprepared for meetings or presentations.

Any or all of these negatives could be held against you when you request a raise, so it's important that you provide your employer with as little negative ammunition as possible that could be used as justification for rejecting your request. If you have a habit of showing up late for work, for example, make sure this does not happen for at least one or two months straight prior to asking for a raise.

TIP

You may find that your superiors are more apt to keep track of negatives and mistakes you make than they are to document your successes and achievements, which is why it's essential that you keep track of your own successes and achievements while on the job.

☆ ☆ WARNING ☆ ☆

Never give your current boss an ultimatum that unless you receive the raise you're demanding you'll quit. A "take it or leave it" ultimatum often won't work, plus you must be 100 percent ready to quit if your plan fails.

Alternatives to Earning a Raise

If you determine that you deserve a raise, but that your employer is not willing or able to pay you what you deserve, try negotiating for improved perks and benefits. As you will learn in Chapter 10, every perk and benefit you're offered has a monetary value associated with it. So if your employer keeps your paycheck the same, but offers you benefits and perks that will save you money or improve your quality of life, this too can be valuable and beneficial.

For example, if your employer will start paying your commuting and parking expenses, this eliminates the need for you to pay these expenses out of pocket using after-tax income. If you're given a bigger employee discount on items or services you'd otherwise pay full price for, this too will save you money.

Another benefit you could potentially negotiate for, in addition to or instead of a pay raise, is additional paid vacation and sick days. Also, if your employer is unwilling to offer you a permanent pay raise, perhaps you could negotiate a bonus-based compensation plan, where you receive a preset cash bonus for meeting specific objectives or goals. If your job involves sales, you could negotiate for higher commissions, as opposed to an increase to your base pay. Once you determine what is and isn't possible in terms of negotiating a pay raise with your employer, use a bit of creativity to come up with variable options that might be acceptable to your employer and that you'd benefit from.

When to Seek Alternate Employment

Unfortunately, no matter how hard you work or how deserving you are of a raise, you may discover that your employer is simply unable or unwilling to pay you more, offer you a promotion, or in any way compensate you for the added value you're providing to your company that's above and beyond the basic responsibilities of your job. If this is the case, you may have reached a dead-end point working for that employer. You may discover that you offer more value in the job marketplace than your employer is willing to admit, and it may now become necessary for you to seek alternate employment opportunities in order to truly begin earning what you deserve.

TIP

Even if you're happily employed and believe you're being fairly compensated, always keep your eyes open for new and better job opportunities. While you don't necessarily have to be an active job seeker, if you hear about a better-paying opportunity you'd qualify for, it might make sense for you to pursue it (confidentially, of course). In the business world, opportunities tend to reveal themselves when they're least expected and when you aren't necessarily looking for them.

Chapters 7, 8, and 9 focus on finding new, higher paying employment opportunities. If this is the path you decide to follow, however, it's an excellent idea to begin your job search and obtain at least one job offer before you quit your existing job. This not only keeps a steady paycheck coming in, but also gives you ample time to find the right opportunity without feeling rushed. Simply quitting your job without having a new one lined up is rarely, if ever, a smart career move.

How to Ask for a Raise

Based on what you've learned from this chapter and the salary related research you've conducted, if you've discovered that you deserve a raise and there's a good chance your employer will consider your request, there's definitely a right way and a wrong way to ask for that raise. The next chapter focuses on how to get the raise you deserve. If you believe you deserve a promotion, as well as a raise, be sure to read Chapters 4 and 5.

CHAPTER 3

Earning **a Raise**

WHAT'S IN THIS CHAPTER

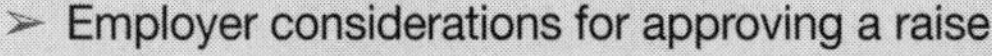

- Employer considerations for approving a raise

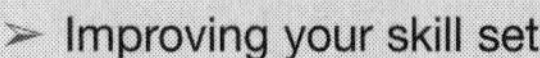

- Improving your skill set
- How to request a raise
- When to request a raise
- How to negotiate your raise
- Biggest mistakes to avoid when requesting a raise
- When your raise request gets rejected
- Is a promotion in your future?

Determining in your own mind that you want *and* deserve a raise is only the first step toward earning a higher income for doing the work you're already responsible for based on your job title and position within the company you're employed by. The next step involves asking your employer for a pay increase, and then convincing your superiors you're worthy of receiving it. How you ask for a raise, when you ask, and how you demonstrate worthiness of receiving a raise will all impact your ability to get your request approved.

There are basically two types of raises. One is based on merit, performance, and achievements—it's earned. The other type of raise is a cost-of-living increase (typically between 3 and 5 percent) that your employer automatically awards once per year, for example, to some or all of its employees.

This chapter focuses on how and when to ask for a merit-based raise, and offers strategies for improving your chances of getting your request approved. Remember, deciding you want

TIP

If your request for a raise is denied by your superiors, never make any rash decisions about how to proceed and don't take the employer's decision personally. At the end of this chapter, you'll learn strategies for dealing with having your raise request rejected.

and deserve a raise does not mean your employer will agree or be able and willing to grant your request when you make it.

Employer Considerations for Approving a Raise

A variety of circumstances will be evaluated before you're granted the raise you request. Some of the things your employer will consider include

- how long you've been working for the company;
- whether paying you more will increase the value you offer to the company;
- the abundance (or scarcity) of qualified applicants available to replace you (people with your overall qualifications);
- the overall financial well-being of the company;
- what other people within your company with similar responsibilities are earning;
- what the average income is for someone with your overall qualifications within your industry;
- when you received your last pay increase;
- whether you're worth more money than you're currently being paid;
- whether or not you've exceeded, not just met, the responsibilities and expectations of the employer, based on your job description;
- your attitude, dedication, attendance record, and productivity; and
- your past work-related performance and overall merit.

Most of the time, when an employer offers you a pay increase, it's not because of your popularity within the company. It also has little or nothing to do with how much your boss likes you personally. In fact, the decision about whether to grant you a raise is rarely, if ever, personal. Whether or not a company is willing to pay you (one of its employees) more is typically a financial and business decision that has to do with the company's profitability, future goals, management philosophy, and your overall performance.

Often, a raise is given to an employee as a reward for achieving a significant goal or objective that benefited the company. What an employer will seldom care about is why you want a raise. In other words, the employer doesn't care about the debt you've racked up, or that you are behind on

☆ ☆ WARNING ☆ ☆

Possessing an advanced degree, such as a master's in business administration, does not automatically command a higher salary in today's competitive job market. In many cases, your advanced degree will be nothing more than a prerequisite for being considered for a job. A degree only indicates that you have job performance potential. What most employers seek are people with proven experience and achievements. These things make you a more valuable asset to an employer.

your bills, have recently taken on a mortgage or new car payment, or need additional money to pay for your child's education. Your personal financial situation is probably of no interest whatsoever to your employer.

What is of interest to your employer is how your work helps the company earn more profit, meet its deadlines, overcome the challenges it's facing, and achieve its goals. Chances are, you fit into one of the following categories from your employer's perspective:

You're someone who does little or nothing more than the bare minimum in regard to what's expected of you based on your existing job description. Thus, getting your request for a raise approved could be difficult.

You've developed a reputation for consistently going above and beyond what's expected of you, based on your responsibilities and job description. This makes you a more viable candidate for a raise.

As an employee who works for someone else, you have the responsibility to look out for your own best interests—professionally and financially. Obviously, when you request a raise, it's for your own best interest. A good strategy for actually obtaining a raise, however, is to always look at things from your employer's perspective. While you'll want to have a clear reason in your head for requesting the raise and understand how you will benefit, part of your preparation before asking for a raise should be to develop a plan that allows you to sell your employer on the idea, based on how it will benefit them.

The easiest way to sell your employer on the idea of granting you a raise is to provide detailed qualitative and quantitative examples of your successes and achievements while on the job, and showcase exactly why your employer will be able to expect even bigger and better things from you in the future. Once again, you want to focus on the value you provide to your employer.

Improving Your Skill Set

By now you should realize two things about your *personal skill set*. First, it's what separates you from others because it's unique to you. Your unique combination of skills allows you to meet the requirements of your job and handle the responsibilities given to you.

TIP

Even if you've won the "Employee of the Month" award several times in a row, or you're clearly the most successful salesperson working for your company, never assume that your superiors already know everything that you contribute on an ongoing basis in an effort to exceed what's expected of you and excel at your job. At the time you ask for a raise, you'll want to recap your greatest successes and achievements, plus reaffirm why you're worthy of a raise. Be ready to provide specifics, including relevant dates, facts, figures, and statistics.

Second, your skill set is one of the key things that make you valuable to your employer. It not only allows you to do what you were hired to do, but it also gives you the potential to take on new challenges and responsibilities. When a potential employer is deciding whether or not to hire you, or when your existing employer is contemplating whether or not to grant you a raise or promotion, they will look closely at your skill set.

Personal skill set. This is the unique combination of skills you possess that allows you to meet all of the responsibilities related to your job. Your skill set pertains to the collection of individual skills you have, as well as your proficiency using each of those skills in the real world. Reading a book to enhance your public speaking skills, for example, will teach you the basics of that skill. You'll need to spend time practicing and fine-tuning the skill, however, before you become highly proficient using it on the job. Every job or position requires a different combination of skills. An employer's goal is to match up job requirements with people who have the proven skills necessary to meet the demands of each position.

TIP

In addition to your personal skill set, an employer will focus on your education, work-related experience, attitude, merit, and past performance when evaluating you as an employee and considering whether or not to grant you a raise.

Depending on what type of work you do and what industry you work in, different employers will put different values on specific skills. Core skills, like reading, writing, and math are taught in school. Few schools teach people how to use these and other extremely important skills in the business world, however, and that includes graduate schools offering business degrees.

Some of the core skills that are in high demand in most industries and by most employers include the following:

- *Computer literacy.* The ability to use a computer to handle some of the responsibilities related to your job. Depending on the work you do, this might include using a computerized cash register, or it could mean being proficient using Microsoft Office or other specialized computer programs.
- *Listening skills.* Your ability to focus on, consider, and potentially act on what other people have to say involves listening. This includes taking direction from your superiors, interacting with co-workers, and being able to communicate well with customers, clients, and others you do business with.
- *Reading skills.* The ability to read and understand a wide range of written materials, from books and manuals, to all forms of correspondence, such as e-mails, faxes, and traditional letters and memos, is often essential.
- *Verbal communication skills.* Your ability to communicate with others in person and over the telephone is also an important business skill. This includes public speaking,

and potentially possessing top-notch customer service or sales skills.

- *Writing skills.* Your ability to communicate in writing, using the written word—on paper and via e-mail—is also an essential business skill to possess.

In addition to these core skill groups, many employers look for more specific skills and personality traits. By developing these skills in the right combination to meet the needs of your employer, you could dramatically enhance your value, plus increase your chances of getting hired and then earning a raise or being awarded a promotion.

Some of the important skills and personality traits useful in today's business world include the following:

Analytical thinking
Arbitrating
Brainstorming
Budget management
Buying
Coaching
Computer literacy
Controlling
Coordinating
Creating
Data entry
Designing
Diagnosing
Drawing
Editing
Entertaining
Fundraising
Innovating
Investigating
Leading
Listening
Meeting planning
Multilingual
Multitasking
Negotiating
Order taking
Organizing
Planning

Policy making and enforcing
Problem solving
Public speaking
Researching
Scheduling
Selling
Supervising
Telemarketing
Time management
Training
Troubleshooting
Typing
Web page design

TIP

It's up to you to acquire the skills and personality traits that are important, and then adapt them for use in your line of work.

Speaking of personality traits, how would you describe yourself as an employee? Take a moment to think about this. Then consider how your employer would describe you if an employee evaluation or performance review pertaining to you was being written today. Take a look at Figure 3.1: Positive Skill/Personality Trait Score Card. At least a dozen of the traits listed should describe you. If not, and if you want to make yourself a more valuable employee (which in turn will increase your chances of earning the raise you want), then it's up to you to develop or improve upon the following skills and traits that relate to you and the work you do.

FIGURE 3.1: POSITIVE SKILL/PERSONALITY TRAIT SCORE CARD

On a level of one to five—with one (1) meaning you do not possess the skill/personality trait at all, and five (5) meaning you possess this trait and are highly proficient using it—rate how many of the following personality traits and skills you possess and to what level. For at least a dozen of these items, you should be able to give yourself a four (4) or five (5) score. To properly evaluate yourself, also consider how your employer would rank you; and be honest.

When it comes time to selling your skill set and personality traits to employers, you'll want to focus on those that you believe you're highly proficient using and that directly relate (or could relate) to your job responsibilities.

Skill/Personality Trait	**1** (Nonexistent)	**2**	**3**	**4**	**5** (Highly Proficient)
Adaptive	❑	❑	❑	❑	❑
Aggressive	❑	❑	❑	❑	❑
Alert	❑	❑	❑	❑	❑
Always on time	❑	❑	❑	❑	❑
Articulate	❑	❑	❑	❑	❑
Attentive	❑	❑	❑	❑	❑
Attractive	❑	❑	❑	❑	❑
Cheerful	❑	❑	❑	❑	❑
Clean cut	❑	❑	❑	❑	❑
Competent	❑	❑	❑	❑	❑
Computer literate	❑	❑	❑	❑	❑
Creative	❑	❑	❑	❑	❑

FIGURE 3.1: POSITIVE SKILL/PERSONALITY TRAIT SCORE CARD, CONT.

Skill/Personality Trait	1 (Nonexistent)	2	3	4	5 (Highly Proficient)
Deadline-oriented	❑	❑	❑	❑	❑
Dedicated	❑	❑	❑	❑	❑
Dependable	❑	❑	❑	❑	❑
Detail-oriented	❑	❑	❑	❑	❑
Dresses professionally	❑	❑	❑	❑	❑
Dynamic	❑	❑	❑	❑	❑
Effective	❑	❑	❑	❑	❑
Efficient	❑	❑	❑	❑	❑
Enthusiastic	❑	❑	❑	❑	❑
Experienced	❑	❑	❑	❑	❑
Flexible	❑	❑	❑	❑	❑
Follows directions	❑	❑	❑	❑	❑
Friendly	❑	❑	❑	❑	❑
Goal-oriented	❑	❑	❑	❑	❑
Good humored	❑	❑	❑	❑	❑
Good listener	❑	❑	❑	❑	❑
Hardworking	❑	❑	❑	❑	❑
Highly social "people person"	❑	❑	❑	❑	❑
Honest	❑	❑	❑	❑	❑
Internet savvy	❑	❑	❑	❑	❑
Intuitive	❑	❑	❑	❑	❑

FIGURE 3.1: POSITIVE SKILL/PERSONALITY TRAIT SCORE CARD, CONT.

Skill/Personality Trait	1 (Nonexistent)	2	3	4	5 (Highly Proficient)
Leader	❑	❑	❑	❑	❑
Motivating	❑	❑	❑	❑	❑
Multilingual	❑	❑	❑	❑	❑
Outgoing	❑	❑	❑	❑	❑
Polite	❑	❑	❑	❑	❑
Productive	❑	❑	❑	❑	❑
Professional	❑	❑	❑	❑	❑
Reliable	❑	❑	❑	❑	❑
Self-starter	❑	❑	❑	❑	❑
Sincere	❑	❑	❑	❑	❑
Stable	❑	❑	❑	❑	❑
Success driven	❑	❑	❑	❑	❑
Superior verbal and written communicator	❑	❑	❑	❑	❑
Tactful	❑	❑	❑	❑	❑
Takes responsibility for actions	❑	❑	❑	❑	❑
Team-oriented	❑	❑	❑	❑	❑
Trustworthy	❑	❑	❑	❑	❑
Unique	❑	❑	❑	❑	❑
Well-rounded	❑	❑	❑	❑	❑

Now let's take a look at your potential negatives. What are the qualities or traits you possess and exhibit at work that could keep you from earning a raise or promotion? What is it that people (particularly your superiors, co-workers, customers, and clients) dislike about you? Take a look at Figure 3.2 and determine which of the following negative traits apply to you.

Using a scale of one to five—with one (1) meaning the trait does not exist or doesn't apply, and five (5) meaning it's a trait you strongly possess and exhibit on a regular basis—consider how your superiors would evaluate you.

When reviewing this checklist, your goal is to honestly be able to rank yourself with a number one or two for each item. Depending on your employer, possessing any or all of these traits could hold you back from earning a raise or promotion, or it could even be grounds for dismissal. If you find that you possess a handful of these traits and you're displaying them on the job often, consider seeking help to overcome and eliminate them quickly.

If you currently exhibit any of these negative characteristics (or have in the past), you can expect your employer to bring them up during an employee evaluation or performance review, or when you request a raise or promotion. If you're in the process of changing jobs and a potential employer contacts your previous employer for a recommendation, are any of these negative characteristics likely to come up and be held against you?

☆ ☆ **WARNING** ☆ ☆

Possessing any or all of these negative traits and regularly displaying them while on the job will cause you to create a negative professional reputation for yourself. While it's easy to establish a negative reputation, it's extremely difficult to fix it, so pay attention to how others perceive you.

FIGURE 3.2: NEGATIVE PERSONALITY TRAIT SCORE CARD

Skill/Personality Trait	1 (Nonexistent/ Does Not Apply)	2	3	4	5 (Strongly Possess and Often Exhibit While on the Job)
Annoying	❑	❑	❑	❑	❑
Arrogant	❑	❑	❑	❑	❑
Backstabber	❑	❑	❑	❑	❑
Bigoted	❑	❑	❑	❑	❑
Careless	❑	❑	❑	❑	❑
Consistently late	❑	❑	❑	❑	❑
Depressing	❑	❑	❑	❑	❑
Difficult to understand	❑	❑	❑	❑	❑
Dishonest	❑	❑	❑	❑	❑
Disorganized	❑	❑	❑	❑	❑
Does not follow directions	❑	❑	❑	❑	❑

FIGURE 3.2: NEGATIVE PERSONALITY TRAIT SCORE CARD, CONT.

Skill/Personality Trait	1 (Nonexistent/ Does Not Apply)	2	3	4	5 (Strongly Possess and Often Exhibit While on the Job)
Doesn't take responsibility for actions	❑	❑	❑	❑	❑
Immature	❑	❑	❑	❑	❑
Ineffective	❑	❑	❑	❑	❑
Inefficient	❑	❑	❑	❑	❑
Insincere	❑	❑	❑	❑	❑
Irrational	❑	❑	❑	❑	❑
Irresponsible	❑	❑	❑	❑	❑
Liar	❑	❑	❑	❑	❑
Loud / outspoken	❑	❑	❑	❑	❑
Mean	❑	❑	❑	❑	❑
Narrow-minded	❑	❑	❑	❑	❑
Nasty	❑	❑	❑	❑	❑
Obnoxious	❑	❑	❑	❑	❑
Poor (ineffective) written or verbal communicator	❑	❑	❑	❑	❑
Poor communicator	❑	❑	❑	❑	❑
Poor dresser (unprofessional appearance)	❑	❑	❑	❑	❑
Poor listener	❑	❑	❑	❑	❑
Pretentious	❑	❑	❑	❑	❑
Racist	❑	❑	❑	❑	❑

FIGURE 3.2: NEGATIVE PERSONALITY TRAIT SCORE CARD, CONT.

Skill/Personality Trait	1 (Nonexistent/ Does Not Apply)	2	3	4	5 (Strongly Possess and Often Exhibit While on the Job)
Rude	❑	❑	❑	❑	❑
Self-centered	❑	❑	❑	❑	❑
Selfish	❑	❑	❑	❑	❑
Sexist	❑	❑	❑	❑	❑
Short-tempered	❑	❑	❑	❑	❑
Shy	❑	❑	❑	❑	❑
Uncooperative	❑	❑	❑	❑	❑
Unprofessional	❑	❑	❑	❑	❑
Unreliable	❑	❑	❑	❑	❑

How to Request a Raise

The first step *before* requesting a raise is to determine what the specific policies are within your company for doing this. Also, determine whether or not your company offers raises based on merit. Check your employee manual or with the human resources department for this information.

If your company has a specific method or process you should follow when requesting a raise, be sure to follow it exactly. Don't improvise or try to outsmart or circumvent the system. Doing this demonstrates that you are *not* able to follow company policy and directions. Also, be sure to follow the hierarchy or chain of command within your company. If, for

TIP

Chapter 4 focuses on how to improve your skill set to make yourself a more valuable employee. This can be done by participating in on-the-job training, pursuing additional education, reading books and training manuals, watching training videos, attending adult education classes, seeking the help of a co-worker or superior and using them as a mentor, using distance learning programs (including online courses), attending seminars given at trade shows, participating in internships, or somehow gaining additional work-related experience.

example, you answer to a manager or supervisor, start by setting up a meeting with this person to request your raise. Don't go over their head unless you're specifically told to do so. Your superior may say they have no control over salaries, in which case you should then ask whom you should speak with.

Keep in mind that many employers have policies that allow for raises to be awarded only at specific times of the year. In this case, asking for a raise any other time would be counterproductive. Some companies have fixed salary ranges or pay grades that are enforced, meaning that managers or supervisors are not able to award raises because the salary an employee receives is determined by their job title or position within the company. It's important to determine how your company operates before going through the process of asking for a raise.

Without a doubt, the best way to request a raise is to do it in person—not in the form of a written letter or e-mail. Even if this process invokes a lot of stress or your boss tends to intimidate you, it's important that you maintain a professional and upbeat attitude throughout the process. Asking for a raise in person promotes dialogue and two-way communication. If your request for a raise is denied, you can determine why and inquire about what it would take to be considered for a raise in the future.

Choose a time to ask for a raise when you know your boss (and you) will have a light schedule. Ideally, you should set up a meeting with your superior in advance, preferably in an informal environment (as opposed to in your or their office). When you set up the meeting, state that you want to discuss your work performance, achievements, and compensation.

After you've set up a meeting with your superior, begin to plan your strategy for requesting your raise. (This strategy

☆ ☆ WARNING ☆ ☆

If your company's policy clearly states that it does not award merit-based raises, your chance of receiving one is virtually nonexistent. If you want to make more money, you'll need to earn a promotion, which means taking on a new job title with additional (and perhaps varied) responsibilities. See chapters 4 and 5 to discover strategies for requesting and earning a promotion.

TIP

Often, your immediate boss, manager, or supervisor will not have the authority to grant you a raise independently. In many situations, your superior will need to forward your request (along with their recommendation) to their superior(s) for approval before your request can be granted. Understanding how this process works at your company will make it go smoother.

will depend on your relationship with your superior, as well as other factors.) Prepare for the meeting and be able to support the claim that you *deserve* to earn more money. Focus on your achievements and successes, including the following:

- The amount of new business you've brought into the company
- The challenges you've helped your company overcome
- The customer satisfaction you've helped the company generate
- The deadlines you've been responsible for helping the company meet
- The extra (unpaid) hours you've invested working for the company on a voluntary basis
- The important projects you've helped to successfully complete
- The increases in productivity you've helped to generate

- The initiative you've demonstrated in taking on responsibilities that are above and beyond what was expected of you based on your job title or position within the company
- The money you've helped the company save
- The qualities, skills, and experiences that set you apart from your co-workers (in a positive way)
- The revenue you've helped the company earn
- The solutions to problems you've helped the company successfully implement
- The specific ways you've helped to improve the products or services your company offers
- The staff training and development you've helped to facilitate

As you develop your presentation and list of successes and accomplishments, be sure to focus on the benefits your employer has received as a result of your hard work and dedication. Always focus on what's important to your employer.

TIP

When showcasing your successes and achievements to your employer during your meeting, be sure to provide specific examples. Don't just talk in general terms.

When to Request a Raise

There are definitely better times to ask for a raise than others. In many cases, timing is critical for achieving a positive result. The following is a list of the best times to request a raise, assuming your company is open to considering such requests anytime:

- During or immediately after you receive a positive employee evaluation or performance review
- After you have successfully achieved a significant goal, deadline, or milestone working for the company
- After the company has experienced a strong financial quarter or year (and you can demonstrate your contribution to that success)
- When you determine your boss or superior is in a good mood
- After you've held your current position (with the same employer) for at least six months to one year (or longer)

☆ ☆ WARNING ☆ ☆

Asking for a raise when your boss is overwhelmed, dealing with a crisis, or facing a particularly busy time of year will hurt your chances of success. Likewise, refrain from requesting a raise if your company has just experienced financial losses during the previous quarter or year. Also, if your company's policy is to offer raises once per year, only at a specific time of year, don't bother requesting your raise at any other time.

☆ ☆ **WARNING** ☆ ☆

Upon doing your salary related research, if you determine you're already being paid higher than fair market value for your work, you'll probably have a difficult time getting a raise approved. Consider pursuing a promotion instead.

Determining How Much of a Pay Increase to Request

The question of how big a pay raise to request can only be answered by doing research. The amount should depend on the average salary paid by your employer to people with similar job responsibilities, the company's policy for setting salaries, the average salary of someone with your qualifications within your industry and your geographic area, current market conditions, and the financial stability of your company. The most important factor, however, is your current and potential value as an employee. Refer to Chapter 2 for advice on doing salary related research.

How to Negotiate Your Raise

When speaking with your employer about obtaining a raise, try using the following ten negotiation strategies to help bring about a favorable result:

1. Know exactly what you want going into the negotiation, but be willing to listen to what your employer

wants and needs. Listening and compromising are two of the keys to a successful negotiation.

2. Go into the meeting fully prepared, with all of your research printed out and documented.
3. Establish a dialogue (two-way communication) where you can state your ideas, opinions, wants, and needs, but also allow your employer to do the same.
4. Make sure you understand your company's procedures for requesting a raise and also what its policies are for granting one.
5. Determine, in advance, how much of a raise you're looking for. Have a number in mind (based on the research you've conducted) and be prepared to negotiate for it and to justify it. Make sure what you're asking for is realistic.
6. Be willing to take on additional job responsibilities if given a raise (even though you'll retain the same job title and position within the company).
7. Focus on more than just your salary. Often, it's easier for your employer to award you additional perks or benefits based on merit (all of which have a financial value) than it is to authorize a pay raise.
8. Never go into a salary meeting or negotiation expecting to receive everything you want. Be realistic. Be open to compromises that provide a win-win solution for you and your employer.

9. Be prepared to have your request for a raise rejected. If this happens, ask why. Also, ask what you could begin doing differently to make yourself eligible for a raise in the future. Be sure to inquire when an appropriate time to revisit your raise request would be (typically three, six, or 12 months down the road).
10. While you're focusing on your positive attributes and contributions, be prepared for your employer to bring up your negatives. For example, if you're consistently late for work or lack follow-through on important obligations, this might be a reason for your employer to reject your raise request. Be prepared to deal with this. One excellent way to handle negatives is to refrain from demonstrating any negative behaviors for a period of several months prior to asking for a raise.

TIP

If your request is rejected and you learn that the employer isn't willing to offer a pay raise to someone in your position, try negotiating for better perks or benefits. If this too fails and indication is given that your future requests will also be rejected, you have two main options—pursue a promotion or quit your job after seeking out a new employment opportunity.

Biggest Mistakes to Avoid When Requesting a Raise

There are many reasons why your request for a raise might get rejected. Some of these reasons may deal directly with you as an employee and whether or not you deserve the raise you request, while other reasons may have to do with the timing of your request, the financial strengths of the company, or circumstances that are beyond your control.

To reduce the chance that your request for a raise will be rejected, take the following advice:

- Never request a raise because you're experiencing financial problems. When you're asked why you deserve a raise, don't say it's because your landlord raised the rent, or you want to buy a new car. Your employer is not responsible for or interested in your money management or budgeting problems.
- Never lose your temper or act unprofessionally during your meeting, especially if things don't seem to be going smoothly or as expected.
- Don't go into a meeting to ask for a raise unless you are well prepared. Failure to understand your company's policies and procedures related to how raises are granted is a huge mistake and one that can be easily avoided.
- If you discover a co-worker is earning more than you are, don't use this as your primary reason for asking for a raise. This does show, however, that your employer has flexibility in terms of pay ranges. Figure out what

you need to do in order to be deemed worthy of earning a higher salary. Focus on your merits, successes, accomplishments, skills, and potential.

- When asked how much of a raise you're looking for, don't request an amount that's unrealistic or that's more than someone higher up than you earns. Again, conducting salary related research in advance can help you avoid this common mistake.
- Never show signs of negativity or of being disgruntled with your employer, co-workers, work environment, or anything related to your job when requesting a raise. This is a time to focus on the positives.
- Don't give an ultimatum. This is unprofessional behavior and ineffective, especially if you have no intention of following through with your ultimatum, such as a threat to quit.
- Understand the terms of your employment. If you were told when you were hired that you'd be evaluated for a raise in one year and you agreed to this, don't start demanding a raise after just three or six months on the

☆ ☆ **WARNING** ☆ ☆

Never surprise your superior by spontaneously requesting a raise. Be sure to schedule a meeting in advance.

job. Pay attention to the company's policies and guidelines and adhere to them exactly. Going against these policies and guidelines could negatively impact your chances of receiving the requested raise.

When Your Raise Request Gets Rejected

Unfortunately, just because you believe you deserve a raise and ask for one, your employer might not grant your request—at least not immediately. So, be prepared to have your request rejected and have a plan in place to deal with that reality.

If your raise request gets rejected, find out why. Ask questions and pay attention to the answer(s) you're given. Determine what you need to do, starting immediately, to qualify for or be considered for a raise in the future. Also, figure out when you should consider making your request again, assuming you continue to exceed the expectations of your employer in terms of meeting your job-related responsibilities and performance.

Once you know what needs to be accomplished and what's expected of you, it's much easier to give your employer what's asked for in order to earn your raise. If you determine your raise request was rejected due to company policy, decide whether it's in your best interest to pursue a promotion instead. If, however, you don't qualify for a promotion (and won't anytime soon), and it's made clear there is no raise coming in your future, you can either stay in your existing job (at

> ☆ ☆ **WARNING** ☆ ☆
>
> If your request for a raise gets rejected, always act professionally. Unless you plan to quit your job as a result, you'll still need to work with these people on an ongoing basis and you don't want to embarrass yourself or create an uncomfortable work environment.

your current salary) or start pursuing other job opportunities with other employers.

Remember, the decision to award a raise is typically based on a person's merit and performance—not personality. So if your request is rejected, don't take it personally. It's probably not because you're disliked. For whatever reason, you simply did not meet the guidelines the company uses to award a raise at the time you requested one. Take another look at the "Employer Considerations for Approving a Raise" section of this chapter and determine which of these situations applied when your employer rejected your request. Next figure out what you could do, if anything, to remedy the situation within the next three to six months.

Is a Promotion in Your Future?

The processes of asking for a promotion and requesting a raise are somewhat similar, although the outcomes are different. Earning a raise or promotion is typically based on merit and performance. While earning a promotion usually includes being awarded a raise, it also means taking on a new job title, being given additional responsibilities, and potentially moving forward along your career path.

The next chapter focuses on determining if you deserve a promotion, and discusses what it will take to earn one based on your current employment situation. Chapter 5 then explores how to actually go about requesting a promotion from your existing employer.

CHAPTER 4

Do You Deserve **a Promotion?**

WHAT'S IN THIS CHAPTER

- Wanting vs. deserving a promotion
- Determining what position you could fill
- Meeting a new job's responsibilities
- Acquiring necessary skills
- Pros and cons of being promoted
- Landing the promotion you deserve

In Chapter 2, you were asked a simple question, "Do you deserve a raise?" You also learned the difference between a *raise* and a *promotion*. The premise of this chapter is whether or not you deserve a promotion and have the skills, experience, and knowledge to earn one. Once again, it's important to understand that there's a huge difference between simply *wanting* a promotion and *deserving* one—based on your merit, performance, accomplishments, skills, education, and experience.

There are three types of promotions, which are described as follows:

- *Standard promotion.* This is when your existing employer gives you a new job title, more responsibilities, and a pay raise. You may also receive additional perks and benefits. The promotion represents a step up the proverbial corporate ladder, and typically means your employer will now have higher expectations for you in terms of performance.
- *Lateral promotion.* This type of promotion offers new responsibilities and a different job title, but isn't accompanied by a pay raise, nor does it necessarily represent a step up the corporate ladder. It could simply mean a job change or transfer from one department, group, or division within your company to another.
- *New job promotion.* Sometimes, to receive the recognition and compensation you truly deserve, it's necessary to change employers and pursue alternate opportunities. This type of promotion involves leaving your existing job and being hired by another employer to fill a more

advanced position than your previous one. Your new job would come with a more impressive job title, higher pay, and additional responsibilities. You'd qualify for this job based on your overall qualifications and past performance. You might pursue a new opportunity in order to achieve career advancement if your existing employer refuses to promote you when a promotion is deserved.

Here the focus will be on determining if you deserve a promotion and on the pros and cons associated with obtaining the promotion you both want *and* deserve. Once you determine you have what it takes to earn a promotion, you can learn about how to earn it by reading Chapter 5.

Wanting vs. Deserving a Promotion

Earning a promotion means taking on a new job title. The new job will also come with new and additional responsibilities. Once again, before you're awarded a promotion, your employer will consider several factors, including

- your past performance and achievements;
- your seniority with the company;
- whether you're the best person for the job;
- your existing skills, experience, and education;
- the value you'll offer to the employer;
- whether you're worth the salary associated with the new job;
- your future potential; and
- your personality and dedication to the company.

A smart employer will consider each of these factors carefully and choose the right applicant to fill the job opening. Knowing what your employer will consider and what's important to the decision makers will make it easier for you to showcase yourself as the ideal person for the job as you strive to meet the employer's demands. One of the best ways to discover what your employer is looking for is to carefully read the job's description, plus use what you already know about the company's management philosophies.

If you've achieved success working in a lower-level position, your objective should be to convince your employer that you have what it takes to successfully handle the responsibilities of what a higher-level job will require. While some employers have a policy to hire from within, others are open to bringing in new people from outside the company in order to fill available positions. This makes earning a promotion that much more challenging, because you must position yourself as the most qualified candidate for the job among a larger pool of potential applicants.

Wanting a promotion means you desire more money, responsibilities, and power within the company. Deserving a promotion, however, means you've already proven yourself to the employer, you have the qualifications to fill the higher-level position, and you're willing to apply for and do what's necessary to pursue a promotion in order to move your career forward. This means being able and willing to meet the new requirements and expectations of your employer.

To help convince your employer you're worthy of a promotion and not just a raise, be prepared to answer the following questions and provide quantifiable examples relating to your past work-related accomplishments:

- How much new business have you brought into the company?
- How have you helped increase productivity?
- What impact have you had on the company's overall success?
- What special projects have you been a part of that have contributed to the company's success?
- How much unpaid overtime have you put into your job within the past three to six months?
- What sets you apart from your co-workers?
- What makes you a viable applicant for the higher-level position you're seeking?

☆ ☆ WARNING ☆ ☆

If you're not willing and able to work longer hours, take on greater responsibilities, or meet the expectations that are associated with the higher-level job you're seeking, don't pursue the promotion. Obtaining a promotion and then failing to meet the requirements of the job could result in your dismissal or a demotion—either of which are detrimental to your long-term career.

- What will be your greatest strengths when it comes to meeting or exceeding the responsibilities and expectations that come with the promotion you're seeking?

Determining What Position You Could Fill

Determining you want and deserve a promotion is definitely the first step in the process. The next important step is to determine exactly what new, higher-level, and higher paying job you're qualified to fill within your company. It's much easier to step into an existing and available position within your company than it is to convince your employer to create a new position or job title specifically for you.

TIP

When seeking a promotion, focus on what you know the employer is looking for, then use your past performance working for that employer as your ammunition for positioning yourself as the most qualified person for the job. Whenever an employer is forced to fill an open position, they take a risk on whom they hire and hope that person will have what it takes to meet the employer's needs and expectations. The more you can do to reduce the risk for your employer, the better your chances of landing a promotion will be.

TIP

If, based on your research, you determine you're not yet qualified or ready to take on a higher-level position within your company, don't pursue a promotion. You don't want to waste your employer's time considering you for a job you're not qualified to fill. A better strategy is to take the steps necessary to become qualified, and then pursue the promotion at the appropriate time.

To determine what position or job title to pursue, study your company's corporate hierarchy. Once you pinpoint what job title or position you're interested in filling, do research to determine exactly what's required of someone in that position. Your employee handbook will be a valuable resource. You might also want to chat with someone who already holds the position you're striving to fill. Read the job description and applicant requirements carefully. The hope is that what you offer and what's required will be a perfect match. If not, it becomes your responsibility to create a perfect match by improving your education, skill set, and work-related experience as needed.

Every job title or position within a company has predefined qualifications, employer expectations, and responsibilities associated with it. Based upon what you know about yourself and your qualifications, it's essential that you pinpoint what job title and position you're qualified to fill. You might determine that you don't have what it takes to earn a promotion right now, but with a few month's worth of training, education, or extra work, you could become qualified to fill a higher-level position and earn that desired promotion.

Within a company, similar job titles within different departments might have vastly different requirements associated with them. Your research will help you determine what job title or position you'd potentially be qualified to fill as you pursue a promotion. After pinpointing this, you'll need to determine if the company has any openings for that job title and position, and when the best time would be to apply for the position.

TIP

As soon as you believe you're ready and able to take on additional responsibilities within your company and want to pursue a promotion, have a formal discussion with your supervisor, manager, or superior about your desires. Even if no higher-level positions are currently open, you can determine exactly what your employer would be looking for from you in order to consider you for a promotion. If, in your employer's opinion, you're lacking something that would be required for a promotion, you can use this information to improve your overall offerings by enhancing your skill set, for example.

Meeting a New Job's Responsibilities

Upon learning what the responsibilities of the job you want entail, first determine whether or not you are capable of meeting those responsibilities, and then convince your employer. By applying for a promotion, you are acknowledging that you believe you're not only qualified to meet the responsibilities of the higher-level position, but also willing to take on those new and additional responsibilities.

In most situations, applying for a promotion involves many of the same steps as applying for a new job with a new employer. Even though your employer knows who you are, depending on the size of the company, as well as its management philosophies and policies for granting promotions, you'll typically need to formally apply for a promotion and participate in one or more employee evaluations or performance reviews. It will become your job to sell yourself, along with your accomplishments, successes, and merit to the employer.

Match up what the job requires with what you have the ability to offer, comparing each required skill, one at a time, if necessary. Keep in mind that accepting a promotion requires a significant commitment on your part. Are you at a point in your life and career where you're willing and able to make this commitment, or would you prefer to stick with your existing job and perhaps pursue earning a raise as opposed to a promotion?

You may determine that you are ready to pursue a promotion, but you are not qualified enough to earn it. If what you're lacking (from your employer's perspective) is work-related experience, there's little you can do to overcome this except try to sell your potential, plus put in the time to acquire the necessary on-the-job experience. If, however, you determine it's your education or skill set that's lacking, you can take immediate actions to begin remedying this situation by pursuing on-the-job training or more education. The next section of this chapter focuses on how to go about improving your skill set and education.

Be sure to review the Positive Skill/Personality Trait Score Card featured in Chapter 3 and determine how each positive skill and personality trait you possess could be applied to the position you'd like to fill should you be granted a promotion.

Acquiring Necessary Skills

The skills and education you'll need to acquire before being considered for a promotion will vary greatly based on your occupation, the job title and position you're pursuing, your employer, and the industry you work in. Common methods you could use to improve your skill set, education, overall qualifications, and value to your employer are outlined below.

Keep in mind that scholarships, loans, tuition reimbursement, and other financing options may be available to help you cover the costs associated with improving your education and training. In addition to making a financial investment in your future, you'll also need to invest the time and effort needed to pursue any or all of the following options. This may require working at your existing job on a full-time basis, plus

TIP

Read the job description for the position you hope to be promoted to carefully. Compare the required skills with the skills you already possess, and then determine the best way to demonstrate your proficiency to your employer using each required skill. Never assume that just because you've been working for that company for several years that the person responsible for approving your promotion will be familiar with your work, reputation, and accomplishments.

investing some of your evening hours or free time on weekends or during vacations to pursue the education or training you want and need.

You will discover that night and weekend classes are offered through many colleges, universities, and adult education programs. Plus, if you use training videos or online-based distance learning programs, the coursework required can be done at your own pace and around your existing schedule.

Once you determine what knowledge or skills you want and need to acquire, figure out the fastest, most cost-efficient way to obtain what's needed. Some of your options include:

- *Return to school on a full-time or part-time basis.* You could return to school either full time, part time, or take night or weekend classes at a local college, community college,

TIP

If you're thinking about returning to school, be sure to visit the Free Application for Federal Student Aid (FAFSA) web site (www.fafsa.ed.gov) to determine eligibility for scholarships or loan options from the government (at the federal and state levels). This is a more cost-effective way to finance your education than through private loans from banks or lending institutions. Contrary to popular belief, at least some government scholarship money or low-interest students loans are available to virtually anyone who wants to continue their education at an accredited school, college, or university.

vocational school, or university in order to earn an advanced degree or certification.

- *Pursue on-the-job training.* Many employers offer on-the-job training on a voluntary, paid, or unpaid basis. Consider pursuing whatever training is available to you, especially if the training can be completed during your existing work schedule. The more training you receive, the more valuable you'll become to your employer (and to future employers).
- *Read "how-to" books.* Just as you're reading this book to learn how to land a raise or promotion, you can read other "how-to" books that teach every imaginable skill.

While some books will help you obtain the academic knowledge you need at your own pace, you'll still need to put your newly acquired knowledge to work in the real world. Some skills are easy to acquire, but can dramatically improve your value to an employer and increase your ability to do your job more effectively and efficiently.

- *Watch training videos or DVDs.* Some people learn better by seeing and hearing content and information, as opposed to reading it. If you're one of these people, watching training videos or DVDs or listening to audio books is an excellent way to learn new skills at your own pace.
- *Attend instructional seminars.* Trade shows are an ideal place for attending seminars. Seminars can be used to learn a wide range of different skills from experts in a short time. Most seminars last only one or two days, and some last just a few hours.
- *Participate in distance learning (online) programs.* Many accredited schools, vocational programs, colleges, and universities now offer distance learning programs via the internet. At your own pace, you can watch lectures, complete coursework, and take required exams—all from the comfort of your home or office (or anywhere with an internet connection). These programs tend to be less expensive than courses you would take in person, plus they can be completed at your own pace. The drawback is that you must be motivated to do all of the

work, because there's nobody taking attendance or ensuring that you keep up with the program you sign up for.

- *Take adult education classes.* Many cities offer adult education classes on a wide range of topics. If you need to become proficient using a computer software application or want to learn a new skill, taking an adult education class requires a minimal time commitment and is typically much less expensive than taking a college course.
- *Participate in an internship or apprenticeship.* Participating in an internship or apprenticeship allows you to learn directly from people with experience while being in the

☆ ☆ WARNING ☆ ☆

Before registering for a distance learning program, make sure the school or institution you'll be studying with is accredited and that you'll receive credit for your work. Your efforts should lead to a legitimate and widely recognized certification, degree, or diploma. The ClassesUSA web site (www.classesusa.com) is one source for learning about a handful of distance learning programs from accredited schools. Yahoo! Education (http://education.yahoo.net/degrees/index.html) is another excellent resource for learning about and comparing distance learning programs.

real world doing hands-on work. The biggest drawback is that most internships or apprenticeships are unpaid (or participants are paid very low wages). Thus, it's best to participate in this type of program while you're still in school. If you're a member of a trade union or professional organization, a formal apprenticeship program may be available. Most high schools, colleges, and universities have established internship programs in place with many different employers.

- *Learn from one or more mentors.* No matter what career path you're following or what industry you work in, chances are you could benefit from having a professional mentor. This is someone who has already accomplished more than you professionally, has a higher-level job title, or has more work-related experience than you do. It's someone who can offer you guidance, advice, instruction, and expertise in an informal way, whenever it's wanted or needed. A mentor is typically a friend as well as a superior who takes a personal interest in you and your career.

Pros and Cons of Being Promoted

Don't just assume that earning and accepting a promotion will be the answer to all of your career-related goals and dreams. Before pursuing or accepting a promotion, consider carefully all of the pros and cons. It's best to create your own written pros and cons list.

The following are potential pros for pursuing and accepting a promotion. Place a checkmark next to each one that applies to your own situation and the promotion you're pursuing:

- ❑ Pay raise (higher income)
- ❑ Better perks and benefits
- ❑ More autonomy (less supervision from your superiors)
- ❑ Additional authority
- ❑ More flexible work schedule
- ❑ More enjoyable work-related responsibilities
- ❑ Bigger office
- ❑ Elimination of (or ability to delegate) work-related tasks you don't enjoy
- ❑ A step forward along a career path

TIP

Once you receive an offer for a promotion, make sure the overall compensation package you'll be receiving is adequate to cover the additional responsibilities and workload you'll be taking on. Again, this is where salary related research becomes important, as does knowing what you deserve to be earning and what perks and benefits are important to you.

Now let's look at the potential drawbacks associated with accepting a promotion. Again, place a checkmark next to each one that applies to your own situation:

- ❑ Longer work hours
- ❑ More responsibilities
- ❑ Greater work-related stress
- ❑ Tighter deadlines to meet
- ❑ Less free time (or less time to spend with family and friends)
- ❑ More people to supervise or manage
- ❑ Heavier workload
- ❑ More work-related travel required
- ❑ Significantly higher expectations from your employer
- ❑ More stress or pressure to meet the demands of the job
- ❑ The need to juggle more tasks and responsibilities simultaneously

Landing the Promotion You Deserve

By now, you should have decided whether or not you want a promotion, and also whether you deserve a promotion. Based on your research, you should know exactly what job title and position you want to fill, and be able to determine what will be required of you if you pursue and ultimately land the promotion.

After considering all of this, including the pros and cons associated with accepting a promotion, you should know whether you're still interested in landing a promotion (as opposed to keeping your existing job, pursuing a pay raise, or seeking out a new job with a new employer). If you are, then read the next chapter to learn how to pursue and ultimately land the promotion you both want and deserve.

CHAPTER 5

Landing a Promotion

WHAT'S IN THIS CHAPTER

- Getting your employer's attention
- How and when to ask for a promotion
- Mistakes to avoid
- Negotiating your new salary and compensation package
- Your career path and future
- Acing employee evaluations

Just like asking for a raise, requesting a promotion is a multistep process—one that you should be fully prepared for before you approach your supervisor or boss. Based on the information within the previous chapter, you should already know the following:

- What you want in terms of a raise or promotion
- Based on your past on-the-job performance and successes, you deserve a promotion
- What specific new job title and position you're interested in obtaining within your company
- You're fully qualified to fill a higher-level position
- What the new job would entail based on the job description offered by the employer, your research, and conversations with other employees where you work
- The policies and procedures your employer follows for granting promotions
- The pros associated with the higher-level job outweigh the cons
- You're willing and able to accept the new responsibilities and challenges of the job, plus meet or exceed your employer's higher expectations
- The higher-level job you want is or will soon be available
- The approximate salary and compensation package you'd be looking for if given the position you desire (based on your research)

Once you have all of the necessary information available to you, the next step in obtaining a promotion is to formally approach your employer to request it. The process for doing this is much like asking for a raise (see Chapter 3). You'll want to adopt a highly professional approach by setting up an in-person meeting with your boss, preparing (in advance) all of the materials and information you'll need to convince your employer that you are the best candidate to fill the higher-level position, and then participating in a job interview–like meeting before your employer makes a decision. If offered the promotion, you'll then need to engage in a salary negotiation and carefully evaluate the job offer prior to accepting the new position.

Here you will find strategies for pursuing the promotion you desire, assuming the timing and conditions are right and that you are fully qualified for the higher-level job you want to pursue.

☆ ☆ WARNING ☆ ☆

Timing almost always plays a huge role in whether or not you'll be awarded the promotion you want and deserve. For example, there's no point in pursuing a promotion if the higher-level position you want is not currently available and there's no indication it will become available in the near future. Pay attention to the timing of your request, what challenges your employer is currently facing, and what their policies and procedures are for offering promotions from within.

Getting Your Employer's Attention

In the weeks or even months prior to formally requesting a promotion, transform yourself into an employee who already has earned that promotion. What this means is that you should work to eliminate any and all doubt that may exist in your boss's mind that you're fully qualified for the job. Start dressing in a way that's appropriate for the higher-level job you want. Your appearance is important to many employers. If you're seeking a managerial or supervisory role, for example, adopting a more professional, clean-cut appearance will help demonstrate your dedication.

Know that while you're focusing on your positive qualities and professional strengths, your employer will also evaluate your negatives, based on your prior job performance. Some of the things you can start doing now to position yourself as a "model employee" include the following:

- Do more than just the bare minimum in regard to your current job requirements. Take the initiative and strive to always exceed the employer's expectations.
- Take on new responsibilities and begin learning how you'd handle the higher-level job you desire.
- Show up for work on time and don't take extended lunches or coffee breaks.
- Adhere to the company's dress code—consider dressing for the higher-level position you want, not the one you currently have.
- Adopt a more positive and outgoing attitude.

- Follow all directives from your superiors, as well as your company's policies and procedures.
- Attend and be fully prepared for all mandatory meetings, and when appropriate become an active participant.
- Demonstrate your managerial skills when appropriate.
- Handle yourself in a highly professional manner, especially when dealing with your superiors, co-workers, customers, and clients.

By taking these actions (and any others you deem appropriate), you should be able to get your employer to notice you

TIP

One of the best ways to prove you're capable of handling the responsibilities of a higher-level position is to take on those responsibilities when someone currently in that position takes a vacation, goes on maternity leave, takes a short-term leave of absence, or calls in sick. Be able to demonstrate that you can successfully step in and take on the responsibilities of the job you're hoping to land through a promotion. This can be a very persuasive tactic. Seek out opportunities to prove yourself that will also allow you to learn how to handle other people's job responsibilities as well as your own. The more you know about the company's overall operations, the more valuable you become as an employee.

and that will be reflected in your next employee evaluation(s). Regardless, it's still important for you to always maintain a written diary of your accomplishments, achievements, and successes while on the job.

Showcase Your Skills, Accomplishments, and Successes

In your work diary, keep track of what you do, how you do it, specific dates, what skills you use, and most importantly, how the results of your actions and contributions benefit your employer. When it comes time to be evaluated for a possible promotion, it will be your past performance, your value as an employee, and what the employer perceives your future contributions could be that will determine the outcome of the decision.

To help you document all of your contributions and keep track of relevant data, consider making an achievement worksheet to complete your work-related diary. Remember to keep copies of all nonclassified reports, letters of recommendation, correspondence with superiors, and other data that can be used to showcase your achievements.

Based on your months or years in your current position, you should be able to create a detailed and somewhat extensive diary of your accomplishments and contributions that go above and beyond your core job responsibilities. While you'll want to present this information to your employer when asking for a raise or promotion, you do not need to share your actual written diary. This should be a reference tool you use to help you gather relevant information and data that support the idea that you deserve (and have earned) the promotion you're requesting.

How and When to Ask for a Promotion

If you're lucky, your employer will notice the incredible work you do and all of your contributions to the company. Thus, when a higher-level position opens up within the organization, you will automatically be considered for that job without you having to do anything but accept the offer. That's what happens in a perfect world. We all know, however, that the world we live in is less than perfect. So in most cases, to obtain the promotion you want and deserve, you'll need to take the initiative and pursue it.

Just like when requesting a raise, there's definitely a right way and a wrong way to request a promotion, and timing is often a critical component in the employer's decision-making process.

When considering you for a promotion, your employer will look at the following:

- How long you've been working for the company
- Whether paying you more and giving your more responsibility will increase your value to the company
- Your qualifications and how they match up with the requirements for the higher-level position
- The current abundance (or scarcity) of qualified applicants available to fill the higher-level job

- The overall financial well-being of the company
- What the average income within the industry is for someone with your qualifications
- When you received your last promotion
- Whether the employer perceives you have untapped potential that could be exploited by giving you more responsibilities
- Whether you've exceeded, not just met, the responsibilities and expectations of the employer in the past, based on your current job description
- Your attitude, dedication, attendance record, merit, and productivity
- The company's policies in regard to promoting from within or looking elsewhere to fill its current or upcoming job openings

The first step *before* requesting a promotion is to determine what the specific policies are within your company for doing this. Check your employee manual or with the human resources department for this information.

If your company has a specific method or process for applying for a promotion, be sure to follow it exactly. Don't improvise or try to outsmart or circumvent the system. Doing this demonstrates you can't or won't follow company policies and that is not the attitude you're trying to convey.

When applying for a promotion, follow the hierarchy or chain of command within your company. If you're hoping to land the job held by your immediate boss or supervisor, don't sneak behind their back and approach their superior. This could easily be interpreted as backstabbing and would typically not be looked upon favorably. Don't go over anyone's head unless you're told to do so. Your immediate superior may tell you they have no control over awarding promotions, in which case, ask whom you should speak with or contact the human resources department within your company.

Many employers also have policies in place that allow for promotions to be awarded, but only at specific times of the year. In this case, asking for a promotion any other time would be counterproductive. Determine how your company operates before going through the process of applying for a promotion.

Just as when you are requesting a raise, the best way to pursue a promotion is to do it in person—not in the form of a written letter or e-mail. Requesting a promotion in person promotes dialogue and two-way communication. If your request is denied, you can determine why and inquire about what it would take to be considered for a promotion in the future.

Assuming you know a higher-level position is currently (or will soon be) available within your organization, choose a time to request a promotion when you know your boss and you will have a light schedule. Ideally, you should set up a formal meeting with your superior in advance. When you set up the meeting, state that you want to discuss your future role with the company and that you're interested in taking on additional responsibilities.

Once you've set up a formal meeting with your superior, plan your strategy for actually requesting your promotion. This means properly preparing for the meeting and being able to support the claim that you *deserve* a promotion. Focus on your achievements and successes, including

- the amount of new business you've brought into the company;
- the challenges you've helped your company overcome;
- the customer satisfaction you've helped the company generate;
- the deadlines you've been responsible for helping the company meet;
- the extra (unpaid) hours you've invested working for the company on a voluntary basis;
- the important projects you've helped to successfully complete;
- the increases in productivity you've helped to generate;
- the initiative you've demonstrated in taking on responsibilities that are above and beyond what was expected of you based on your job title or position within the company;
- the money you've helped the company save;
- the qualities, skills, and experiences that set you apart from your co-workers (in a positive way);
- the revenue you've helped the company earn;
- the solutions to problems you've helped the company successfully implement;

- the specific ways you've helped to improve the products or services your company offers;
- the staff training and development you've helped to facilitate; and
- the skills you have that could be beneficial in a higher-level position if you were granted a promotion.

As you develop your presentation and list of accomplishments, be sure to focus on the benefits your employer has received as a result of your hard work and dedication. Always focus on what's important to your employer.

Keep in mind that there are better times to ask for a promotion than others. A combination of the following criteria may have to be met before you're considered for a promotion:

- A higher-level position that you're qualified to fill is currently available (or will soon be available)
- You've recently received a positive employee evaluation or performance review
- You have recently achieved a significant goal, deadline, or milestone while working for the company
- You determine your boss or superior is in a good mood
- You've been in your current position (with the same employer) for at least six months to one year (possibly longer, depending on the position, occupation, and industry you work in)
- You are able to demonstrate that you have the experience, knowledge, and skills necessary to meet the requirements and expectations associated with the higher-level position

TIP

If you work in retail, for example, where there is a lot of employee turnover, it's often easy to earn promotions quickly based on your performance and dedication to the company. Once you reach a managerial role within a retail organization, however, earning promotions becomes more challenging since this often means being promoted to a corporate-level job.

Once you've set up a meeting to discuss the possibility of a promotion with your employer, go into that meeting fully prepared and act as if you're participating in a formal job interview (regardless of how friendly you are with your superiors). For example, dress appropriately for a job interview. Choose an outfit that's consistent with (or slightly more formal than) what you'd wear to work on a daily basis if granted the promotion.

During your meeting, act extremely professional. Don't allow emotions to cloud your judgment or impact your behavior. Also, during your premeeting preparation, try to anticipate the unexpected and be ready to deal with a variety of possible scenarios. Just as you would for a job interview (see Chapter 9), practice participating in mock meetings with your superiors.

Focus on how you'll present your accomplishments, showcase your qualifications, and demonstrate your overall value. How you do this will depend on your personality, occupation, the corporate culture where you work, and the professional relationship you have with your superiors. As part of your meeting, you could do the following:

- Begin an open dialogue during which you convey important information about yourself, your qualifications, and your accomplishments to your employer. You could also address their concerns.
- Create a well-written memo that outlines the key points you'd like to cover during your discussion. Use the memo as an outline of key discussion points, and then provide your employer with a copy of the memo at the conclusion of your meeting. The memo could incorporate backup material supporting your accomplishments, such as copies of sales reports, performance data, and financial data.

☆ ☆ WARNING ☆ ☆

Asking for a promotion when your boss is overwhelmed, dealing with a crisis, or facing a particularly busy time of year will hurt your chances of success. Also, if your company's policy is to award promotions once per year, only at a specific time of year, don't bother requesting your raise at any other time.

- Create a PowerPoint presentation showcasing your successes and how your employer would benefit from offering you a promotion. If public speaking will be a requirement of the job you hope to land, this is an excellent way to show off your verbal communication skills, creativity, and ability to conduct a meeting.

Mistakes to Avoid

Being unprepared for your meeting is probably the worst mistake you could make when approaching your employer and asking for a promotion. Simply stating you want a promotion, but not knowing exactly what position you're qualified to fill, or how your qualifications could be adapted to that new position

> **TIP**
>
> After being offered a new job (including a promotion), take time to carefully evaluate the offer. Make sure that you're willing and able to take on the new job, and that it comes with a fair compensation package. When you're ready to formally accept an offer for a promotion, do so verbally as well as in writing. The written acceptance should maintain a professional and upbeat tone while outlining the basic terms of the offer and what you're agreeing to. In many cases, you'll receive and be expected to sign a new employment contract.

FIGURE 5.1: CURRENT JOB/CAREER ASSESSMENT QUESTIONNAIRE

When approaching your employer for a promotion, some of the common scenarios you might encounter include:

Scenario	How to Handle It
Your employer agrees you're the perfect candidate for a higher-level position that's available and makes an immediate offer.	This is obviously the best-case scenario. Your primary responsibility now is to maintain your composure, take time to carefully evaluate the offer, make sure it's something you're able and willing to pursue, and then accept the offer verbally and in writing.
Your employer is open to the idea of granting you a promotion, but isn't sure you're fully qualified to meet the requirements of the higher-level position.	The best way to handle this scenario is to focus heavily on your past accomplishments, as well as your overall qualifications, skills, and untapped potential. Provide specific examples of how you've successfully served the company in the past, and discuss what you are capable and willing to do in the future. Determine what, if anything, you can do to alleviate your employer's concerns. Discuss if obtaining additional training would be acceptable, for example. Use information from your work diary to gather details about your successes.

FIGURE 5.1: CURRENT JOB/CAREER ASSESSMENT QUESTIONNAIRE, CONT.

Scenario	How to Handle It
Your employer believes you're capable of taking on additional responsibilities and succeeding in a higher-level position, but has no current openings.	In this situation, agree to step in to replace whoever is in that job when they go on vacation or call in sick. Determine if the employer is capable of creating an additional or new position for you, or if you'd have to wait for an existing position to open up. If you have to wait, find out how long the wait might be based on average employee turnover, and then decide whether you're willing to wait it out based on your employer's promise to offer a promotion to you when a position becomes available.
Your employer believes you're capable of taking on additional responsibilities and succeeding in a higher-level position, but doesn't have the financial resources available to pay you a higher salary.	If you encounter this scenario, you have a few options. You can stay in your current job and hope the company's financial situation changes. You can also start looking for a new, higher-level job with another employer. Or, you can agree to take on a new job title and responsibilities for the same pay, but negotiate for better perks and benefits. Use your creativity and establish a dialogue with your employer to create a win-win scenario. Chances are, over the long term, you could benefit by receiving a better job title and being given a chance to learn new skills, even if a short-term financial benefit is not currently available.

FIGURE 5.1: CURRENT JOB/CAREER ASSESSMENT QUESTIONNAIRE, CONT.

Scenario	How to Handle It
Your employer does not have faith in your ability and does not believe you are deserving of a promotion at this time.	If you receive this response upon requesting a promotion, maintain a professional attitude, but ask questions. Determine exactly why your employer believes you're not qualified and ascertain exactly what you could do to rectify the situation. Perhaps the employer would require you to undergo additional training, gain more on-the-job experience in your current position, or remedy any negative performance issues (such as a history of showing up late for work). Find out what would happen if you were to eliminate their objections. Would you be considered for a promotion in the future, or are you stuck in a dead-end job with no upward mobility potential?
Your employer has a policy of not hiring from within and isn't open to the idea of granting you a promotion now or anytime in the future.	Unfortunately, if you find yourself in this situation, you have two main options. You can keep your existing job and accept it indefinitely. Or, you can pursue other opportunities with other employers. It's necessary to accept that you're in a dead-end job with little or no future growth potential with your current employer.

will put you at a significant disadvantage. Don't apply for a job you're not qualified for or one that your employer isn't trying to fill.

When asked why you want or deserve a promotion (which will be one of the first questions out of your employer's mouth), never state that you're having personal financial problems and need more money to pay your bills, cover your living expenses, or pay off your debt. Your personal financial problems are of no concern to your employer.

Focus on the benefits you offer to your employer and how being granted a promotion will be advantageous to your company's profits, productivity, and overall operation. Depending on your position, you may want to focus more on your impact within a specific department, branch, retail location, division, or group within your organization, as opposed to the company as a whole.

When making claims about your past performance, successes, and accomplishments, make sure you can support what you say with specific examples, facts, figures, and relevant

TIP

Be sure to follow the advice in the "Biggest Mistakes to Avoid When Requesting a Raise" section of Chapter 3. Much of the same information applies when requesting a promotion.

TIP

As you discuss how you'd handle your new responsibilities if granted a promotion, never focus on the poor job you believe another person is doing. There's no need to stab a co-worker or superior in the back or speak badly of someone else in order to get ahead. Focus instead on your own merits and potential, how you'll deal with challenges your company is facing, and how you'll be instrumental in helping to achieve your company's goals.

financial data. Never make grandiose claims that your employer will know or be able to determine are lies.

Also, regardless of how the meeting between you and your superior(s) progresses, always stay positive, act professionally, and focus on your primary objectives. Create a win-win scenario, where your employer will reap the benefits of your skills, experience, knowledge, and qualifications, while you'll receive a more impressive job title, better pay, improved perks and benefits, more responsibilities, and the opportunity to advance your career.

Negotiating Your New Salary and Compensation Package

Once you're offered a promotion, you will also most likely be offered a pay raise and an improved benefits package. And you might be eligible to receive additional or better perks.

Remember that every benefit and perk has a monetary value associated with it. Even if an employer doesn't have much leeway when negotiating your salary, it's often possible to negotiate for better benefits and perks, so keep your options open. Chapter 10 focuses on benefits and perks and their monetary value.

Before accepting the new job offer, ask to see a detailed job description so you know exactly what will be expected of you. In more general terms, you can learn about job requirements for specific positions and occupations by accessing the

TIP

If your employer asks what your desired salary is for the job being offered, this indicates that there's room to negotiate. Sometimes employers have predefined salary and compensation packages that go with specific job titles. The person granting the promotion has no flexibility when setting someone's salary. Look for clues from your employer that indicate they're open to negotiate. It's perfectly acceptable to negotiate, but know when it's time to stop and accept what's being offered. There comes a time when an extra $50 a week, for example, isn't worth jeopardizing the entire negotiation. Don't be greedy. Make it clear you're looking for a compensation package that's fair and in line with industry standards and current market conditions.

Occupational Outlook Handbook (www.bls.gov/oco) or the U.S. Office of Personnel Management's web site (www.opm.gov/fedclass/html/gsseries.asp). Your company's employee handbook or human resources department could also be instrumental in helping you acquire a detailed job description for the position you're seeking.

Weigh the pros and cons of the promotion carefully, and then determine if the salary and compensation package is appropriate for the position you're being offered. Performing salary related research will be important in helping you determine this.

During your negotiations, your goal is to create a win-win situation. You want the highest pay possible for doing the least amount of work. Make sure your expectations are realistic. At the same time, your employer wants to pay you as little as possible for doing the most amount of work. Be willing to make compromises and focus on your own short- and long-term goals and objectives. For example, how will you benefit from possessing a more impressive job title than you have now? What will you be able to learn in your new job that you can't learn in your existing one? How will the new position help you achieve your long-term career goals faster? These are the types of questions you'll want to ask yourself.

Also during the negotiations, refrain from making demands or ultimatums. You'll have much better luck making requests, listening carefully to your employer's responses, making intelligent counteroffers, and striving to create that win-win scenario. To accomplish this, your listening skills,

TIP

During your salary negotiation, have in mind a ballpark but realistic salary you'd like to receive. Also, determine what the lowest salary you'd accept would be. Try to get the employer to make the offers. As a starting point, if you're asked how much of a raise you're looking for, add about 10 percent to the salary you'd desire based on your research. This gives you the leeway to accept a counteroffer for less, but that's still within the range you're negotiating for.

patience, and creativity will be put to the test as much as your negotiation skills.

Throughout your in-person meetings and the salary negotiation process, pay attention to your body language. Smile and make eye contact. Sit up straight and focus on projecting confidence. Knowing in your heart that you're prepared for the meeting and qualified for the higher-level job you're requesting will help boost your confidence.

Your Career Path and Future

Each new job or position you accept should demonstrate upward mobility in terms of your overall career path and long-term career objectives. While you want to act as if your primary concern is for the employer's well-being and success, never lose sight of your own wants, dreams, and goals for the future. Consider how pursuing a promotion will benefit you and what impact it will have on your life, your financial well-being, and career. How does it fit into the career path you planned for yourself?

If you accept a promotion now, what will the next step in your career be? When will you want to take that next step forward? How will the new position help you reach that next step? How will the new job impact your quality of life, improve your skill set, better round out your work-related experiences, and make you a more marketable worker when seeking out other employment opportunities?

☆ ☆ WARNING ☆ ☆

If your promotion request is rejected, find out why. Figure out what you can do to remedy the situation in the future, but don't burn any bridges by lashing out with insults. A rash decision to quit, walk off the job, or do anything else that would be considered unprofessional could jeopardize your current and future employment situation and damage your reputation. Even though your request for a promotion was rejected, you may discover in three or six months that the situation is totally different.

TIP

Before accepting any job offer or promotion, consider your own wants, needs, and goals.

Acing Employee Evaluations

Before making the decision to grant you a raise or promotion, your employer will most likely take a look at your past performance and the information that's been included in your past employee evaluations or performance reviews. Knowing how important employee evaluations are in terms of your future, you should always strive to ace them and make the best possible impression. Obviously, the best way to do this is to live up to your employer's expectations and demands in terms of job performance. There are many other things you can do to ensure you receive the kudos you deserve. The next chapter focuses on how to make employee evaluations work in your favor.

CHAPTER 6

Acing Employee **Evaluations**

WHAT'S IN THIS CHAPTER

- What employers evaluate and why
- How and when to request an employee evaluation
- Preparing for an employee evaluation
- Your employer's wants, needs, and goals
- When to consider a job change

More and more companies are realizing that their biggest asset is their employee base. Upon discovering this, they want to create the most productive, efficient, and competent work force possible. One way to achieve this is to conduct periodic employee evaluations or performance reviews. This provides employers with an opportunity to evaluate each employee's contribution to the company and ensure that the work being done by each person is contributing toward achieving the company's overall goals.

Every job or position within a company has a predefined set of responsibilities and employer expectations associated with it. An *employee evaluation* (also referred to as an *annual review, performance review,* or *periodic review*) is a formal meeting during which your boss, supervisor, or superior formally analyzes your recent performance and then creates a written report about you. The document created is then placed in your personnel file and made available to your superiors. Depending on the type of work you do, your company, and the industry you work in, the areas covered by your employee evaluation will vary, as will the frequency of these evaluations.

Employee evaluation / performance review. Conducted by your superior at work, this is a periodic review of your on-the-job performance that becomes a permanent part of your personnel file. By combining an in-person meeting with a written report created by your superior, your employee evaluation is much like a school report card. It's often used as a tool to help an employer determine whether an employee is worthy of receiving a raise or promotion. If an employee's performance, attitude, and work are not measuring up, a negative evaluation can also be used to make the decision to fire, demote, or discipline an employee.

Most employee evaluations are comprised of two components—an in-person meeting with your superior, followed by a written report prepared by your superior that will ultimately be passed along to higher-level management and kept in your personnel file. Every employer's process for handling employee evaluations or performance reviews is different, but it's something that's probably described in detail within your employee manual. It's a process that is taken very seriously by most employers and should be taken seriously by you as well.

From an employer's standpoint, employee evaluations are essential for keeping tabs on each employee's performance

TIP

After (not during) a positive employee evaluation or performance review is completed is often an ideal time to tell your employer you're interested in receiving a raise or promotion. Set up a meeting to discuss your wants and needs. The results of your positive employee evaluation will serve as a tool to help persuade your employer that you're deserving of the raise or promotion you're requesting.

and determining who is doing their job and who isn't. An evaluation is also an opportunity for an employer to address concerns they may have with an employee. From your perspective, an employee evaluation is a time to ensure that your recent successes, achievements, and accomplishments have been noticed by your superiors and that you're receiving proper credit for your work.

While small employers are able to keep a close watch on employees on an ongoing basis, medium-size and large-size companies rely more heavily on employee evaluations—allowing upper-level management to keep tabs on lower-level employees they may rarely come into direct contact with or never actually meet or work directly with.

☆ ☆ WARNING ☆ ☆

If you work for a large company, it will be your immediate superior who recommends you for a raise or promotion, but the ultimate decision will often be made by a higher-level executive within the company who may not know you or be familiar with your work. As a result, they'll rely heavily on the content of your employee evaluations or performance reviews to make their decision about whether to grant you a raise or promotion. This makes the information within these reports extremely important to your future.

What Employers Evaluate and Why

Employers that use evaluations often initiate them quarterly, semiannually, or annually. In addition to overall on-the-job performance, some of the categories that might be evaluated or reviewed include the following:

- Ability to follow directions
- Attendance and punctuality
- Attitude
- Communication skills (verbal and written)
- Competencies
- Concerns the employee may have
- Concerns the employer may have
- Delegation skills
- Dependability
- Ethics
- How well the employee works with co-workers (teamwork)
- Initiative
- Leadership ability
- Overall job knowledge
- Problem-solving skills
- Productivity
- Recent accomplishments
- Recent failures
- The employee's overall impact on the company (positive or negative)
- The employee's relationship with customers and clients

TIP

When you're hired for any new job, determine in advance what will be considered in your employee evaluations, what responsibilities you'll have, and what your employer's expectations of you will be. This will help you ace your evaluations, because you'll know exactly what's expected of you on a day-to-day basis and over the long term.

Typically, for each category that your employer deems important, the person handling your employee evaluation will award you a grade. The grading system is often just like in school, with an "A" representing a top mark and an "F" representing failure. These grades will typically be accompanied by short paragraphs of text describing the recent performance of an employee as it relates to each category.

One of the topics that might be discussed during your employee evaluations is what work-related goals you have for the upcoming period. These might be goals or expectations provided by your employer or ones you've set for yourself, where the outcome relates directly to your job performance.

In many situations, an employer will review your past employee evaluations to make important decisions about your future—including whether you deserve a raise or promotion, or are a liability to the company and should be let go. If your company is facing difficult times and considering downsizing its work force, your positive employee evaluations become that much more critical to your job security.

Simply by meeting or exceeding the expectations of your employer in terms of your job performance and by meeting the responsibilities of your job on a day-to-day basis, you'll have little or no trouble acing employee evaluations.

Consider your employee evaluation or performance review to be equivalent to a school report card. You're being graded and critiqued in an effort to help you better work within the company and improve yourself as an employee.

☆ ☆ **WARNING** ☆ ☆

While an employee evaluation can be used to help you earn a raise or promotion, a poor evaluation from your superior could provide your employer with reasons to fire, discipline, or demote you. Especially if you've already earned several poor employee evaluations in the past, you might want to reconsider your dedication to your job and improve your performance before your employer takes action.

Sample Employee Evaluation Form

Every company will typically create its own employee evaluation or performance review form, based on the criteria it believes are important. Figure 6.1 is a sample form that is probably similar to what your supervisor would complete as part of your employee evaluation. Knowing what's on the form that your supervisor must complete will help you better prepare for the in-person portion of your evaluation or review.

TIP

To help you prepare for your own evaluation or review, take on the role of your supervisor and complete this form about you (from your employer's point of view). You might also ask a co-worker to complete the form about you, so you can learn firsthand how others perceive you.

How and When to Request an Employee Evaluation

Since many employers rely on information in an employee evaluation to make an intelligent decision about whether to grant that person a raise or promotion, if the timing is right, you might consider requesting an evaluation, instead of waiting six months or more for the next one to take place.

When you're hired for a new job, inquire about how often employee evaluations take place and determine if there's a policy or procedure for requesting an evaluation sooner. There are several reasons why you might want to request an employee evaluation instead of waiting for the next scheduled review. Some of these reasons include the following:

FIGURE 6.1: SAMPLE EMPLOYEE EVALUATION/ PERFOMANCE REVIEW FORM

Employee name: ________________________________

Position: ________________________________

Department: ________________________________

Employee ID number: ________________________________

Date of hire: ________________________________

Definitions of Performance Ratings

"O"– Outstanding. Exceptional performance in all areas. Performance is far superior to others. Equivalent to an "A" grade.

"V"– Very Good. Employee exceeds expectations in most position requirements and offers high overall performance. Achieves results on a consistent and reliable basis. Equivalent to a "B" grade.

"G"– Good. Employee is competent and dependable. Properly handles primary job responsibilities and meets basic performance standards. Equivalent to a "C" grade.

"Improvement Needed." Employee lacks the knowledge, skills, or experience to properly handle their job responsibilities and is not meeting the core requirements of their position. Immediate improvement is required. Equivalent to a "D" grade.

"U"– Unsatisfactory. The employee's performance is substandard and not acceptable. Equivalent to an "F" grade.

"N/A"– Not Applicable. Either the category does not apply to the employee's job title and position, or the employee has not held the job long enough for the employer to properly evaluate their performance.

FIGURE 6.1: SAMPLE EMPLOYEE EVALUATION/ PERFOMANCE REVIEW FORM, CONT.

Category	Rating / Grade	Details or Comments
Quality of work. Refers to accuracy, thoroughness, and overall quality of the employee's work.		
Productivity. Refers to the quantity of work completed, as well as the overall efficiency of the employee.		
Job knowledge. Refers to how capable the employee is of completing their work based on their practical and technical knowledge.		
Reliability. Whether the employee can be relied upon to complete their work accurately, effectively, and efficiently.		
Attendance. Refers to the overall attendance record of the employee, how punctual they are, and whether they observe prescribed meal breaks and work breaks.		
Initiative. The employee's willingness to seek out and take on new assignments and additional responsibilities.		
Interpersonal relationships. Refers to how well the employee works with others, including superiors, co-workers, subordinates, customers, and clients.		
Judgment. Refers to the employee's decision-making skills and how well they use their common sense and judgment while on the job.		

FIGURE 6.1: SAMPLE EMPLOYEE EVALUATION/ PERFOMANCE REVIEW FORM, CONT.

In what areas has the employee improved since the previous evaluation? ____________________

____

____

What should be done over the next three to six months to improve the employee's performance? ____________________

____

____

What have been the biggest accomplishments or achievements of the employee since the last evaluation? ____________________

____

____

What goals or future expectations have been set for the employee to work toward prior to the next evaluation? ____________________

____

____

Overall comments: ____________________

____

____

Manager's signature: ____________________ Date: ________

Supervisor's signature: ____________________ Date: ________

Employee's signature: ____________________ Date: ________

- You believe some of your accomplishments have gone unnoticed by your superiors
- Someone else (a co-worker, for example) is taking credit for your hard work and accomplishments
- You believe you're capable of taking on additional work-related responsibilities and want to discuss this with your superiors
- You believe your employer, for whatever reason, is not pleased with your work or overall performance, but you have received no feedback
- You're having a long-term problem at work and have not been able to solve it on your own
- You hope to land a raise or promotion in the near future
- You've been working in your current position for six months or longer, and want to solicit feedback from your employer about your performance

While not everyone is comfortable bringing attention to themselves or their accomplishments, this is essential if you don't believe you're automatically receiving the recognition for your work that you deserve, or you believe someone else is taking the credit for your achievements. Remember, you will only be evaluated on work that's being accredited to you.

The best way to request a formal employee evaluation is to submit a letter or memo (on paper or via e-mail) to your immediate superior that requests the meeting. It should state the reason why you're requesting it. You should only do this, however, if your next scheduled employee evaluation is more than three to six months away, and you have a legitimate reason to request that the evaluation happen sooner. Remember that the reason you provide should be one that's in the best interest of your employer (as well as you). Just because you *want* an employee evaluation next week so you can request a raise is not a valid enough reason why your employer should drop everything and accommodate your request.

Preparing for an Employee Evaluation

Don't wait until a few days before your scheduled employee evaluation to begin preparing for it. Ideally, you want to be working on a daily basis to ensure you're meeting or exceeding the expectations of your employer. What you should do prior to your evaluation meeting, however, is compile your own list of recent successes, accomplishments, and achievements to make sure your employer is fully aware of your contributions, dedication, hard work, loyalty, and overall value as an employee.

If you've been consistently late to work, missed important meetings, or been late meeting deadlines, or your overall performance isn't up to the expected standards, you can bet this will come up during your employee evaluation. When this happens, it's in your best interest to have a well-thought-out response as to why various aspects of your performance have been substandard, and to also have a plan in place to remedy the situation quickly. Never try to lie about or deny information that's accurate but doesn't reflect well upon you. Your best bet is to take responsibility for your actions—both good and bad—and demonstrate a true willingness and ability to improve.

The hope is that any negative criticism or comments your employer has about you and your performance will be greatly outweighed by the positive contributions you've made to the company since your last employee evaluation. Whether or not this is the case, however, is entirely up to you.

Prior to your in-person employee evaluation meeting, consider putting together a series of written lists that describe the following:

- What you have accomplished since your last evaluation
- What you've improved upon since your last evaluation
- What goals you have recently achieved
- What company or division-related problems you have helped solve
- What new or extra responsibilities you're capable of taking on
- What new job-related goals you're interested in pursuing in the future
- What ideas you have on how to improve the overall performance of the company or your division
- What untapped potential you have as an employee

This is all information you'll want to have covered during your employee evaluation in order to make sure your superiors are fully aware of your contributions. Remember, there's no reason whatsoever to get nervous during an employee evaluation—unless you've been slacking off or you're about to get caught for having done something you shouldn't have.

TIP

When compiling your lists of accomplishments and contributions, divide them into two categories—things you have achieved that are already part of your job responsibilities, and accomplishments and contributions that are above and beyond what was actually required or expected of you. This first category is essential for keeping your employer happy with you. The second category is what will play a huge role in helping you earn a raise or promotion. Refer to your job description to help you compile each list and categorize your contributions appropriately. Again, this is information you'll want to bring to your employer's attention.

The goal of the in-person portion of your evaluation should be to ensure that you and your employer have a meeting of the minds in terms of your responsibilities and what the employer's expectations are of you. For you, this is an opportunity to build a more personal bond with your superiors, prove your value, demonstrate your potential, and develop future goals that will help your company, but also assist you in moving forward on your career path.

Treat the in-person portion of your employee evaluation as the important business meeting that it is. Dress and act professionally, go into the meeting fully prepared, and be willing to accept whatever criticism or feedback is offered. This criticism and feedback should be used as a tool to help you better meet the expectations of your employer in the future and better understand the responsibilities of your job. Whatever happens, never take what's said to you as a personal attack or react to criticism or feedback unprofessionally—by yelling or insulting your superior, for example. Always maintain your composure.

If something comes up during your employee evaluation that's inaccurate or that you disagree with, bring it to your employer's attention. Request a break if necessary so you can gather documentation that supports your version of the facts.

Your Employer's Wants, Needs, and Goals

An employee evaluation is the perfect time for you to reaffirm to your employer that you're a dedicated, hardworking employee who is loyal and has the best interest of the company in mind. As you outline your own contributions, successes, and accomplishments, put them into a context that demonstrates how you have assisted the company in achieving its goals. For example, discuss what you have done to improve overall performance, sales, revenues, productivity, customer service, and teamwork within your company or your division within the company.

Focus on how you're helping to make your company stronger and how your skills, knowledge, and experience allow you to help the company overcome its challenges and obstacles. Obviously, it's important for you to have and pursue your own career-related goals. For the purpose of an employee evaluation, however, you want to structure your

> ☆ ☆ **WARNING** ☆ ☆
>
> If you're lucky enough to have developed a personal friendship with your superior, who happens to be the person responsible for completing your employee evaluation, do not rely on that friendship and expect your superior to lie for you or embellish the truth when conducting your evaluation. This could easily put their job in jeopardy, and it's an unfair request to make to a true friend.

own goals so they appear consistent with your company's. After all, your employer's first and foremost concern is with the strength, well-being, profitability, and success of the company as a whole. The wants, needs, and goals of individual employers are typically of secondary concern to the employer.

As you describe your accomplishments and contributions, put them in terms that demonstrate how your employer came out ahead. For example, you can discuss how your leadership skills have allowed the company to earn 15 percent higher revenues in the past quarter, or how your talents have generated a 10 percent increase in sales, thanks to all of the new business and additional clients you've generated.

If, for example, you know that one of your company's goals is to increase overall productivity by 20 percent over the next six months, discuss how you will work to make this happen. Use some of your past accomplishments as examples, while at the same time showcasing your skills and talents.

Just as you would during a job interview, use your employee evaluation as a way to set yourself apart from your co-workers in a positive way. Stress how you have been and will continue to be instrumental in helping the company achieve its goals and overcome whatever challenges it's facing.

When to Consider a Job Change

Regardless of what industry you work in, the concept of having total job security and remaining employed by the same company from the time you graduate from school until the time you retire is virtually unheard of these days. At various times during your career, you will have to change jobs and seek out new employment opportunities.

There may be times during your career when the decision to change jobs gets made for you—because you get downsized or fired, or your employer goes out of business. Other times, however, you may take the initiative and voluntarily leave your job in order to pursue a better, more lucrative opportunity, or one that will help you advance your career.
The next chapter focuses on helping you decide when and how to seek out new job opportunities and ensure that you don't get stuck in a dead-end job.

CHAPTER 7

Seeking Alternate **Employment Options**

WHAT'S IN THIS CHAPTER

- Seeking a better job opportunity
- How and where to find a better job
- Moving to another city
- Job searching while you're still employed
- When and how to quit your current job
- Start applying for jobs

There are times in nearly everyone's professional life when changing jobs becomes essential for achieving their long-term career and financial goals. Sometimes, these changes are forced upon people when an employer downsizes, goes out of business, or lays off employees as a cost-saving measure. At other times a person may come to the realization that the job they're in isn't leading anywhere, isn't fulfilling or rewarding, and isn't allowing them to reach their goals—financially or otherwise.

Regardless of the reason for changing jobs, there's a right way and a wrong way to do this. The wrong way involves quitting your old job before lining up a new one, or taking shortcuts during your job search so you ultimately wind up accepting a new job that was misrepresented, that has no future potential, or that won't offer the compensation you're looking for. This chapter focuses on finding new employment opportunities that will potentially allow you to earn more than you're currently making, either immediately or in the near future.

There's a difference between changing jobs and changing careers. Going from one job to another means working for a new employer, but in a job where your primary responsibilities are basically the same as they were before. You'll use your existing skill set, education, and experience, and continue to work in your industry or area of expertise. For example, you might go from one retail sales job at the mall to working for another retail store in that same mall. If you're an accountant, you might transfer firms, but maintain basically the same responsibilities. Ideally, however, when you make the job switch, you'll be taking on some additional responsibilities and be able to command a higher salary than before, because the job you'll be taking on represents a step forward in terms of pursuing your career path.

Changing careers is an entirely different matter. This means that not only are you changing employers, but your new job will require you to fulfill a totally different set of responsibilities because you'll be working in a different industry or line of work. For example, you might go from being a retail sales associate to working as a receptionist within a corporate office environment. Changing careers often requires you to obtain additional training and education, and to create a new career path and start from scratch as you work your way up the corporate ladder. For some people, this change represents a new start in their professional life and allows them to refocus their energies on a career they're truly passionate about.

As you'll learn here, when you find yourself looking for a new job, this activity can become a full-time task. It requires time, research, dedication, and plenty of follow-through. Taking a systematic and well-thought-out approach to your job search will help ensure that you ultimately find a job you'll enjoy and that meets your financial wants and needs. If, however, you're desperate for a paycheck and need a job quickly, this puts a tremendous amount of pressure on you and could result in you simply accepting the first job you're offered, regardless of its long-term potential.

TIP

If you find yourself suddenly unemployed and desperate for a paycheck, consider working with a temporary employment agency that could place you in a job quickly, but on a temporary basis. This will give you time to properly pursue more viable permanent job opportunities, yet allow you to earn an income at the same time.

TIP

During the time you're unemployed, be sure to apply for whatever unemployment benefits you qualify to receive. This will help lighten the financial pressure as you seek out new employment opportunities. During this time, be sure to tighten your budget until you once again have a steady paycheck. Do not rely on your credit cards to cover your cost-of-living expenses while you're unemployed. This will quickly get you into debt and could cause long-term financial problems that could take years to resolve.

When seeking out new employment opportunities, your goal should be to find your dream job or one that has the ability to help lead to your dream job. It should also offer upward mobility potential, and involve day-to-day responsibilities that you enjoy. Take a look at the Current Job/Career Assessment Questionnaire in Chapter 1. Use your answers to help you pinpoint a job that will offer the salary and benefits you desire, provide a work environment you'll prosper in, and allow you to use your skills, education, and experience to excel.

The more time, energy, and dedication you put into finding your next job, the better your chances will be of finding one you'll be passionate about and that offers the financial rewards you desire. There are many different methods for finding and analyzing new job opportunities. To achieve the best results, use a handful of these strategies simultaneously.

☆ ☆ WARNING ☆ ☆

If you've decided to leave your job voluntarily in order to pursue a potentially better opportunity, invest the time and effort necessary to find the right job. Don't make rash decisions or forego doing proper research, or you could find yourself stuck in a new dead-end job that offers no potential. Also, for a variety of reasons (including financial ones) it's always best to line up a new job first, before quitting your existing job.

Don't simply rely on "help wanted" ads in a particular newspaper, one job-related web site's listings, or a single job fair.

Seeking a Better Job Opportunity

Anytime you switch jobs, for whatever reason, your goal should be to find a new opportunity that's better than your last. This might mean landing a job with a more impressive title, an increased salary, more responsibilities, a better work schedule, or certain improvements that are important to you. The new job you accept should also represent a step forward in your career (or be equivalent to a lateral promotion) and allow you to move closer to achieving your long-term career goals.

As you embark on your new job search, refer to Chapter 2 and conduct salary related research so you develop a thorough understanding of what you should be getting paid based on your overall qualifications, the job title and position you hope to fill, the industry you'll be working in, and your geographic area. Once you start receiving job offers, you'll want to analyze each offer based on its salary and compensation package and what your potential within the company might be.

Once you know how much you should be getting paid based on your research, you'll be able to determine if a potential employer is offering you a fair salary and compensation package. One thing to consider, however, is how quickly you'd be considered for a raise or promotion, assuming that you meet or exceed the expectations of the new employer and excel in your new job.

The first step to finding a great new job is to focus on what you're looking for and what types of jobs you're qualified to fill. Fill out Figure 7.1 to help you narrow down your options.

FIGURE 7.1: JOB SEARCH QUESTIONNAIRE

Use this questionnaire to help you narrow down the types of jobs you're interested in and that you're qualified to fill; then use your responses to help you evaluate a job offer. Once you receive a job offer, compare your responses to the following questions with what's being offered by the potential employer.

What job title or position are you qualified to fill?________________

What industry do you wish to work in?________________________

What type of company would you like to work for?______________

____

What employers are you interested in working for? ______________

____

____

How do you want to be compensated (salary, hourly wage, commissions, etc.)? ______________________________________

____

____

What benefits and perks are important to you (health insurance, retirement plan, life insurance, child care, tuition reimbursement, etc.)?

____

____

FIGURE 7.1: JOB SEARCH QUESTIONNAIRE, CONT.

What primary responsibilities do you want your new job to include?

____

____

What type of work environment would you prefer? _______________

____

Describe your ideal boss or supervisor: ________________________

____

Describe your ideal co-workers: ______________________________

____

What's your ideal work schedule? ____________________________

____

Do you want to work part time or full time? ______________________

How much of a work-related commute are you willing to endure?

____

Are you willing to travel as part of your job requirements? _________

What on-the-job training or education opportunities are you looking for from your new employer? ____________________________

____

____

What potential within the company is available to you through raises and promotions? ________________________________

____

____

As you compare your responses to these questions with a potential job offer, be willing to make compromises based upon what's important to you. For example, would you accept a slightly lower salary if it meant reducing your daily commute by up to one hour per day? Would you accept a higher salary than you received at your previous job if the benefits package wasn't as good or the work environment wasn't what you were looking for? While you can make career-related decisions based exclusively on salary, you should also consider all other aspects of the job and the experience it will offer immediately and in the future.

How and Where to Find a Better Job

Typically, the best way to find a job is through word-of-mouth, since many job openings are never formally advertised. Many employers prefer to find applicants through

TIP

Sometimes a new employer might hire you for a job that offers a slightly lower salary or benefits package, but tell you that if you successfully handle the responsibilities of the job for three months, you'll be granted a raise, and that in six months to one year, you'll be offered a promotion. Always look at the potential of a job offer, not just what you'd be paid starting on day one.

☆ ☆ **WARNING** ☆ ☆

Lying on your resume or during a job interview will not be tolerated by potential employers, who will typically check your references, verify your past employment history, and perform a detailed background check before you're hired. If you're not qualified for a position you've applied for, it will be discovered relatively quickly and you will have wasted your own time, as well as the potential employer's time.

referrals from current employees than through other recruiting practices. Thus, networking should play an important role in your job search. Remember, to avoid wasting your time and energy, focus on applying for jobs you are qualified to fill and ones that, based on your research, you believe are appropriate for you. If in the past you've only held entry-level jobs, you're probably not qualified for and have no experience working in a supervisory or managerial position. Thus, you should not apply for such a position.

To find the best job opportunities available once you pinpoint what type of position you're looking for and are qualified to fill, try using the following resources:

- *Companies human resources departments.* If there are a handful of companies you know you'd be interested in working for, one option is to approach those employers directly. Contact the human resources department at each company and either schedule a meeting or determine what job openings are available and what the company's policies are for accepting resumes and applications. If you already have a contact with someone who works for a company where you'd like to work, be sure to use that contact and have that person make a personal introduction or set up a meeting for you. Many companies post their job openings on their own web sites, so this is an excellent place to begin before contacting a potential employer directly by telephone or sending your unsolicited resume to the human resources department.

- *Career guidance office at school.* Most high schools, trade schools, vocational schools, distance learning programs, colleges, and universities offer a career guidance or job placement office. Here, you'll find information about job openings and resources that can help you land a job. You might also receive help putting together your resume or preparing for a job interview. These services and resources are free of charge to current students (and often alumni), so be sure to take full advantage of them as you embark on your job search.
- *Career-related web sites.* Thanks to the power of the internet, this is your most valuable job search tool—not just for doing research, but also for finding and even applying for jobs. Using the internet, you can sift through

vast databases containing job listings, and post your resume for potential employers to see. There are hundreds of career-related web sites available, and you can visit the web sites hosted by the companies you hope to work for. In minutes, you can search through job openings based on keywords, job title, location, and a variety of other criteria. If you'll be posting your resume online or submitting it to employers via the internet, it should be written to include keywords (as opposed to many descriptive phrases). See Chapter 8 for details on creating a resume. Some of the career-related web sites offer job listings in addition to other resources, such as job search tools, "how-to" articles and career advice, salary information, and the chance to research potential employers. Popular career-related web sites include

- CareerBuilder (www.careerbuilder.com);
- Careers.org (www.careers.org);
- Craigslist (www.craigslist.org);
- Federal Job Search (www.federaljobsearch.com);
- JobBank USA (www.jobbankusa.com);
- The Monster Board (www.monster.com); and
- Yahoo! HotJobs (http://hotjobs.yahoo.com).

- *Headhunters/employment agencies.* These independent agencies work as middlemen between applicants and potential employers. The employers provide detailed information about job openings, and then the headhunters, employment agencies, and recruiters seek out perfect candidates and conduct preliminary interviews in order to narrow down the employer's options to a few qualified candidates. These agencies charge a fee for their services. Some charge the employers (not the applicants). Others charge both the employer and the applicant once a job is filled. Before working with an agency, determine how it gets paid and when, as well as what services it will provide to you (the job seeker).

- *"Help wanted" ads (newspapers/trade magazines).* Newspaper "help wanted" ads often list dozens or even hundreds of job openings in your immediate geographic area. This is an excellent resource for job leads, and it's important that you act on each ad that's of interest immediately. If a "help wanted" ad catches your attention in Sunday's newspaper, respond to it early on Monday morning. If you wait until later in the week, that employer will most likely have already received dozens of resumes from qualified applicants, which puts you at a disadvantage. When responding to a "help wanted" ad, make sure you're qualified for the job before you apply for it. Also, follow the directions in the ad carefully to discover how the employer wants applicants to make contact.
- *Industry magazines, newsletters, and trade journals.* Reading industry-oriented magazines and trade journals offer you, the job seeker, many advantages. Not only will you learn about a specific industry you're

interested in and what the latest trends are within that industry, you'll also discover who the key players are and which companies are hiring. Most industry magazines and trade journals publish job listings. You'll find industry-oriented magazines and trade journals for a wide range of industries either at large newsstands or libraries. The online editions of these publications can often be found on the web.

- *Job fairs.* Job fairs offer an excellent opportunity to meet a handful of potential employers at once, in a relatively casual environment. You'll discover that career fairs are regularly hosted in virtually every city across America. Some focus on entry-level jobs, while others are attended by employers in a specific industry. For example, TechExpo (www.techexpousa.com) hosts job fairs across America that focus on technical, computer-related jobs. Many high schools and colleges host job fairs. Other fairs are advertised in local newspapers or

TIP

To learn about job fairs being held in your region, visit www.employmentguide.com/browse_jobfairs.html or www.careerbuilder.com/jobseeker/careerfairs/.

on career-related web sites. Job fairs provide an excellent networking opportunity. Treat every conversation as if it's a job interview or valuable job lead. Be friendly and professional, be prepared to describe yourself and your goals, ask questions about the employer, and showcase your personality.

TIP

When you attend a job fair, dress as if you're going to a formal job interview, but wear comfortable shoes (since a lot of walking and standing around are typically required). Also, don't forget to bring at least a dozen (or more) copies of your resume. Often, job fairs are attended by human resources professionals trying to hire people immediately. If you're able to make a positive first impression, you could be hired on the spot, or at least get invited to participate in an immediate formal job interview. Before the job fair, prepare a one-minute speech about yourself that highlights your overall qualifications, your goals, and what type of job you're looking to fill. You'll want to rehearse this minipresentation and be able to present it to each potential employer you meet. Be sure to collect a business card from everyone you speak with at a job fair. This will allow you to follow up afterward with a telephone call, e-mail, or letter.

TIP

It's always better to arrive at a job fair early. Show up a few minutes before the scheduled start time. If you wait until the last few hours of the last day of the event, everyone will tend to be tired, less productive, and less willing to listen to what you have to say. You also run the risk of jobs or interview appointment openings already being filled by applicants who showed up earlier.

- *Networking.* Many of the best job openings are never advertised. The way to find out about them is by networking with friends, family members, past co-workers, your school's career guidance office, or even your barber or hairstylist. Let people know what type of job you're looking for and where you'd like to work. Ask people if they know anyone who can help make an introduction for you into a company. Seek out referrals and advice from the people you know. You'll often find that someone you know may know someone else who is aware of a job opening that's perfect for you. Another way to network is to attend trade shows and industry-oriented conferences and introduce yourself to as many people as you can. Explain that you're looking for a job (and what type of job you're looking for) and don't be afraid to ask for referrals or advice. Most employers are more apt to hire someone who comes highly recommended by a current employee, for example, than someone who simply walks in off the street after sending in a resume.

- *Professional trade organizations and labor unions.* Professional trade organizations, associations, and unions are nonprofit organizations made up of employers and employees working in a specific industry. These organizations typically offer job placement services, training opportunities, and databases of related job openings. These job listings might be published online, printed in a trade magazine, or made available to members who call the trade organization or union directly. Trade organizations and unions also hold meetings, seminars, trade shows, and conferences that provide for excellent networking opportunities for job seekers. The training these organizations offer can help you become more qualified to fill specific types of jobs and increase your earning potential.

TIP

A comprehensive online directory of labor unions is available at www.unionism.com/director.htm or www.ilr.cornell.edu/library/research/subjectGuides/laborUnions.html. A directory of professional trade associations can be purchased from Concept Marketing Group (www.marketingsource.com/associations).

Moving to Another City

There are many reasons why a job seeker might consider relocating to another city, the most popular of which is probably to earn a higher salary. Because the cost of living is vastly different in cities across America, employers often set their salary ranges accordingly. Thus, what one employer pays in New York City, for example, could be different from what an employer in Little Rock, Arkansas, pays someone with virtually identical qualifications in the same position.

The demand for different types of jobs also varies by geographic area. So if the local job market is saturated with people with your qualifications, you may find it necessary to move to a city or region where your skills and qualifications will be more in demand.

Some people opt to relocate to another city simply to start fresh. Regardless of the reason, before choosing what city you move to, determine how the cost of living in that city or region will impact you and your income potential. This can be done through basic research. Cost-of-living calculators, for example, can be found on virtually all of the popular career-related web sites, such as the Monster Board (www.monster.com).

Moving to another city will require you to make significant changes in your life. Not only will you be changing jobs, you'll also have to live in a new home, make new friends, and adjust to life in a new city. By default, you'll be leaving your existing friends, co-workers, and possibly relatives behind. Consider how a move will impact you, your family members, and your loved ones. What impact will it have on your children when they need to change schools and move away from their friends? Will your spouse also be able to find lucrative work in the new city? How will the move affect you financially and emotionally?

It's also necessary to consider the potentially significant cost of the move and whether or not your new employer will pay these relocation expenses. If you're a homeowner, will you sustain a financial gain or loss by selling your existing property and buying a new home in the city you're moving to? Based on home prices, the rental market, the local economy, and the cost of living in the new city, you may find you'll be able to afford a much larger and more luxurious home. Or you could discover that you'll barely be able to afford a small condominium or apartment in the city you're planning to move to, even if your salary goes up.

The BestJobs USA web site (www.bestjobsusa.com/sections/GEN-stateselect/index.asp) allows you to research local job markets by state. The Career InfoNet web site (www.careerinfonet.com) allows you to research industry, wage, and employment trends by city and state.

TIP

Planning a move? The Move.com web site (www.move.com) offers a wide range of resources to make the process easier.

Relocating to another city can provide a tremendous and exciting opportunity for you to move your career forward and improve your income. Proper planning and research are essential, however, to ensure you make the right decisions and avoid costly mistakes.

Job Searching While You're Still Employed

It's always best to conduct your new job search while you're still employed. This allows you to continue receiving your paycheck and benefits; it also gives you the luxury of time. You won't have to make rash career-related decisions as you seek out the best opportunity to pursue. While you still have a job, you can feel comfortable turning down job offers that aren't exactly what you're looking for. You can wait until you find the right opportunity before quitting your existing job.

It is possible to conduct a job search while keeping your current job, without your existing employer finding out. To do this, however, you'll need to take precautions. For example, never list your current work phone number on your resume or use your internet access at work to do job research. Also, when you make contact with potential employers, tell them you'd appreciate keeping your meeting and discussions confidential. When it comes time to attend job interviews, you'll want to schedule these during your lunch hour, after work, or on vacation days, always using discretion so you don't tip off your current employer.

Once you receive a job offer, you might want to mention to your current employer what your intentions are and see if

> ☆ ☆ **WARNING** ☆ ☆
>
> If you quit your job prematurely and are forced to live off your savings (or even worse, your credit cards), after a month or two of searching for a job, you might start becoming worried or even desperate to land a new job. This could put you in a position where you'll be more willing to accept a less than ideal offer without doing the necessary research first.

they will match your new job offer in terms of compensation and benefits. Upon telling your employer about your plans, you may be let go immediately, so be prepared for this. The professional thing to do is to give your employer at least two weeks' notice before quitting.

When and How to Quit Your Current Job

As a general rule, you'll want to quit your job by setting up a private meeting with your boss or supervisor in order to give your two weeks' notice. At this time, it's appropriate to submit a written letter of resignation that maintains a professional and upbeat tone.

While your employer may insist that you leave immediately, offering to stay for two weeks or longer is the right thing to do. This allows your employer to find a replacement for you and have you provide basic training for that replacement

☆ ☆ **WARNING** ☆ ☆

Never burn bridges when quitting a job. You never know if you'll need a recommendation from someone in the future and you don't want to tarnish your reputation within the industry you work in.

if necessary. It also allows you to tie up loose ends and complete any projects you're working on.

If you consider yourself a disgruntled employee and want to get back at your employer by quitting without notice and leaving them in the lurch, that's your prerogative. What you'll discover if you think things through, however, is that this won't help you professionally and could actually cause problems for you and your reputation down the road. Your new employer will understand and respect it if you mention that you can't begin your new job for at least two weeks, so that you can give your current employer proper notice.

When you quit, never steal anything from your employer that doesn't belong to you. This includes office supplies, equipment, proprietary or confidential data, client lists, or anything else that violates your employment agreement or the law.

Your existing employer may invite you to participate in an exit interview prior to your departure. During this interview, always be positive, but honest. If you choose to tell the employer why you're quitting, provide constructive criticism. Don't embark on an unprofessional tirade that includes insults or unsubstantiated claims. Always attempt to leave your existing employer on an upbeat note.

Start Applying for Jobs

Unless you get extremely lucky, the job search process is going to be time-consuming and require a lot of work on your part. Understand this from the start and be willing to make the necessary time investment in your future. Then be sure to take a well-planned and organized approach to your efforts. For example, keep a written journal or diary with information about each job you're interested in and ultimately apply for.

Keep track of important details, such as dates of contact, contact names, locations, phone numbers, e-mail addresses, what was discussed during interview or phone conversations, research data about the potential employer, and specifics about the job opening.

TIP

Proper follow-through during your job search is essential. Be sure to thank anyone and everyone who helps you find or land a job by sending them a personalized thank-you note promptly. This includes human resources people who interview you for potential jobs, or anyone who makes a personal introduction on your behalf to a potential employer.

After using the resources outlined here to find the best possible job opportunities, it will be necessary to make contact with those potential employers and start applying for jobs. To do this, you'll need to create and customize your resume for each job, write a personalized cover letter, potentially complete an employment application, participate in one or more job interviews with each employer, and most likely undergo a salary negotiation and background check before actually getting hired.

The focus of the next chapter is on how to fine-tune your resume to highlight your qualifications and credentials so you'll be considered for potentially higher paying jobs. Then, in Chapter 9 you'll learn strategies for participating in job interviews and capturing a potential employer's attention by making yourself stand out from other applicants in a positive way.

CHAPTER 8

Creating Your Resume and Cover Letters

WHAT'S IN THIS CHAPTER

- Steps to finding your next job
- Creating a resume that gets attention
- The electronic resume format
- Writing powerful cover letters
- Writing thank-you notes
- Next, the interview

Your well-written resume can be an extremely powerful job search tool. The purpose of this one-page document is to introduce yourself to a potential employer, summarize your skills, describe your employment history, list your major accomplishments, and outline your educational background. If you're trying to land a new job that offers you greater earning potential, your resume should clearly demonstrate upward career mobility and a defined career path, and showcase your value to a potential employer.

Ideally, your resume should also set you apart from other applicants (in a positive way) and entice a potential employer to invite you to come in for an interview. Your resume has a lot of important responsibilities. Thus, it's important that you create the most well-written, professional-looking, and attention-getting document possible.

Every line within your resume should convey an important piece of information about you, so that when someone

☆ ☆ WARNING ☆ ☆

No matter what, your resume and cover letter should be 100 percent error free in terms of spelling and grammar. These documents should also provide accurate information to potential employers. Misrepresenting who you are or what your qualifications are is one of the biggest mistakes job seekers make.

quickly scans your resume (for less than 30 seconds), they develop a thorough understanding of who you are, what you're qualified to do, and what potential you offer.

This chapter focuses on creating and fine-tuning your resume. You'll also learn how to write powerful and personalized cover letters to accompany your resume when you're applying for a job.

Steps to Finding Your Next Job

Before you start creating or updating your resume, review the many steps involved in finding, applying for, and landing a new job. Finding the right job will take time, energy, research, and commitment on your part. The steps you'll need to focus on for each job you apply for include the following:

1. Pinpoint the type of job(s) you want to pursue.
2. Choose an industry that offers the right job opportunities.
3. Select companies within your chosen industry where you might want to work.
4. Determine what information about yourself needs to be conveyed to potential employers in order to position yourself as the ideal applicant for the job you're seeking.
5. Create a one-page resume that is well written and that showcases all of the information about you that employers want and need to know.
6. Research and find the best job opportunities to apply for. This involves using online career-related web sites, "help wanted" ads, networking, and attending job fairs.

7. Customize your resume for each job you decide to apply for.
8. Create a well-written cover letter to accompany each resume whether you're submitting it by mail or e-mail or dropping it off in person.
9. Follow up after several days with each potential employer after submitting your resume and cover letter.
10. When an employer contacts you or you get invited to come in for a job interview or participate in one over the phone, schedule that interview and then begin preparing for it. Preparation involves practicing how you'll answer interview questions and interact with the interviewer, deciding what you'll wear to the interview, and researching the company you'll be interviewing with.
11. You'll most likely be asked to complete an employment application as you're waiting for the interview to begin. Many of the questions you'll be asked will require information that's already included in your resume and cover letter.
12. Showcase your personality during the interview, as well as your skills, experience, and overall qualifications. Ask intelligent questions and engage in a conversation with the interviewer (your potential employer).
13. As the interview comes to an end or immediately after it, determine what the next step will be. Should you follow up with the employer? Do you need to provide

the employer with additional materials? Will the employer be in touch with you? If so, in what time frame? If it becomes your responsibility to take the next step, make sure you understand what to do and when to do it.

14. Within 24 hours after the interview, send a hand-written and personalized thank you note to the person or people who interviewed you.
15. You may be invited for a second or third interview, or asked to provide additional materials to the potential employer. If the employer is interested in hiring you, you'll receive a job offer. Make sure you ask for this offer in writing and that you understand what's expected of you. Determine exactly how you'll be compensated. This should all be clear before you accept the job offer and start work.

TIP

Until you have a firm job offer from an employer, don't stop your job search. Continue submitting resumes and seeking out opportunities with other employers. The best-case scenario is to receive multiple job offers and be able to choose which one is best for you and offers the most money.

Creating a Resume That Gets Attention

Chances are, it will be the information you include in your single-sided, one 8.5- by-11-inch page resume that will determine whether an employer has any interest in inviting you to come in for an interview and ultimately hiring you. Your resume should summarize all of the reasons why a potential employer should hire you and include specific examples.

As the human resources professional who works for a potential employer reads (or more often simply scans) your resume, typically in 30 seconds or less, they will be looking for it to answer the following:

- What position are you applying for?
- What are your skills and qualifications?
- What work experience do you have that directly relates to the job you are applying for?
- Are you worth the salary the job pays?
- What will you bring to the company that other applicants can't or won't?
- How will hiring you benefit the company?
- Will you be able to help the company solve the problems it is facing or better achieve its goals?

Your resume is a tool that should help you make a positive first impression on a potential employer. The primary goal of your resume is to peak a potential employer's interest in you. Based on that interest, you may get invited to participate in a job interview, which is your main opportunity to showcase who you are and what you're all about.

If you read any book about how to write a resume, you'll learn there are several popular and commonly accepted resume formats. As an applicant, it's important that you adhere to one of these formats, the most popular of which is the *chronological resume format*.

Chronological resume format. Using this widely accepted resume format, the applicant lists their employment history and education experience in reverse chronological order. This means your most recent jobs, for example, get listed first. This type of resume divides each category of information into sections, such as objective, employment history, education, and skills.

Unless you have unusual circumstances surrounding your employment history or are using the internet and e-mail to submit resumes, it's a good idea to adhere to this resume format, which describes your work history and education in reverse chronological order. Using this format, you can easily demonstrate upward or lateral mobility in your career path based on the job titles or positions you've held.

Figure 8.1 is an example of how a chronological resume should be formatted. Of course, you'll have to incorporate your personal information into each section of the resume as it's appropriate.

Strategies for Creating Your Resume

The following ten strategies will help you create a resume that contains the information employers are looking for:

FIGURE 8.1: SAMPLE RESUME: CHRONOLOGICAL FORMAT

Your Full Name
Street Address, City, State, Zip
Phone Number / Cell-Phone Number
E-Mail Address

Objective: Place a well-written, one- or two-sentence summary of your accomplishments and your career objective here. This information should be targeted to the job title or position you are applying for. Avoid being generic.

Work Experience

200# - Present Your Job Title Employer, Employer's City, State

A one-sentence description of your responsibilities.

- Using three to five bullet points, include short, concisely written accomplishments (listed one at a time). Use facts and figures to support your statements.
- List a second accomplishment.
- List a third accomplishment.
- List a fourth accomplishment. Since this is your most recent job, include more information about it. For subsequent jobs, you will list fewer bulleted points. Be sure to list any awards or recognition you've received, and highlight skills you used to succeed in each job.

19## - 200# Your Job Title Employer, Employer's City, State

A one-sentence description of your responsibilities.

- Using two to four bullet points, include short, concisely written accomplishments (listed one at a time). Use specific facts and figures to support your statements.
- List a second accomplishment.

19## - 19## Your Job Title Employer, Employer's City, State

A one-sentence description of your responsibilities.

- Using two to four bullet points, include short, concisely written accomplishments (listed one at a time). Use specific facts and figures to support your statements.
- List a second accomplishment.

FIGURE 8.1: SAMPLE RESUME: CHRONOLOGICAL FORMAT, CONT.

Education
School Name (City, State)
Highest Degree Earned, Graduation Date
Major
(List each school separately, and include all degrees, honors, credentials, certifications, and licenses earned.)

Certifications and Licenses
This is an optional section of your resume where you can highlight any specialized training, certifications, or licenses you've earned that relate directly to your field.

Military Service
Use this section of your resume to describe your military experience. Many employers respect people who have served in the U.S. military and place great value on the training and discipline it offers.

Professional Affiliations
If you are a member of professional organizations or trade unions that directly relate to your occupation or the job you're pursuing, be sure to list your membership in these organizations and any special titles you hold.

Skills
Using one- or two-word phrases, include a short list of five to ten skills you possess that you know will be used in the job you're applying for and that the employer is seeking. This section of your resume is simply a short list, with each item separated by commas.

1. Start by writing answers to the following questions: What are your skills and qualifications? What work experience do you have that directly relates to the job you're applying for? What can you offer to the employer? How will hiring you benefit the employer? Can you help solve problems or challenges that the employer is facing? What sets you apart from other people applying for the same job? Answering these questions will help you determine what information to include in your resume.
2. The main sections of a resume are as follows: Heading, Job Objectives, Education, Accreditation and Licenses, Skills, Employment History, Professional Affiliations, and Military Service. Choose what information to include under each heading. The actual wording for each resume section can be modified. Also, only include the sections that apply to you.

TIP

Contrary to popular belief, it is not necessary to state at the bottom of your resume that references are available upon request or to actually list your references. You can provide your list of references when you participate in an interview or complete an employment application.

TIP

If you're creating a resume from scratch, consider reading a book about writing resumes to learn more about proper formatting and phrasing. Or try using resume creation software, such as WinWay Resume Deluxe ($39.95, WinWay Corporation, www.winway.com).

3. In the resume's heading, include your full name, address, telephone number(s), fax number, cell-phone number, and e-mail address. If you're trying to keep your job search a secret from your current employer, don't list your work telephone or fax number.
4. When listing your education, don't include your grades, class rank, or overall grade-point average, unless this information is extremely impressive and will help to set you apart from other applicants. The first piece of information listed in the education section of your resume should describe the highest degree you've earned or are in the process of earning.
5. To decide what work experience to include on your resume, start by listing all of your internships, after-school jobs, summer jobs, part-time jobs, full-time jobs, and volunteer or charitable work. Be prepared to provide specific dates of employment, job titles, responsibilities,

☆ ☆ **WARNING** ☆ ☆

One of the most common mistakes people make when creating a resume is not including a phone number where a potential employer can contact them. List a phone number that has an answering machine or voice mail, so someone can leave you a message anytime. You're better off listing a home number or cell-phone number, as opposed to your work number.

and accomplishments for each position. How you convey this information in your resume is critical. You may have to refrain from including some of the less pertinent information in order to conserve space. Never list past salaries earned.

6. As you sit down to write your resume, use action words, which are usually verbs that make your accomplishments sound even better, without stretching the truth. What your resume says about you, and more importantly, how it's said, is what will make your resume a powerful job search tool. Focus on using highly descriptive and powerful words to describe responsibilities and accomplishments. For example, "highly proficient using Microsoft Word" sounds more impressive than "word processing experience."
7. Choose a resume format that best organizes your information for an employer. Using a chronological format is

TIP

When listing your employment history, demonstrate a clear career path and upward (or lateral) mobility with each job listing. For example, if you work in retail, showing your previous job titles as "sales associate," "senior sales associate," "assistant manager," and then "manager" shows a steady progression along a career path. Being able to show this will dramatically help you land a new job that pays more or that's equivalent to a promotion over your last job in terms of job title.

the most common. Your employment experience is listed in reverse chronological order, with your most recent job listed first.

8. Keep your resume short and to the point. Make sure all of the information is well organized and stated as succinctly as possible. Remove redundant words and phrases. You do not need to use full sentences in the bulleted lists within your resume.
9. Print your resume on good quality, white, off-white, or cream-colored paper. Use 24-pound or 28-pound bond paper made of 100 percent cotton stock. Your finished resume should look neat and well balanced on the page. It should be inviting to the reader and not look cluttered. Use white space on the page to make your resume visually appealing and uncluttered.

10. Before distributing your resume to potential employers, proofread it carefully. Even the smallest spelling or grammaticall error will not be tolerated and could result in you missing out on a job opportunity.

Spending extra time on your resume is an excellent investment in your future. Pay careful attention to detail, and make sure that your resume promotes you in the best possible way. To assist in formatting and designing your resume, consider using specialized resume creation software. Since the design and formatting of a resume is just as important as what it actually says, consider reading one of the many books available that explain and demonstrate the resume creation process.

The Electronic Resume Format

An electronic resume is one that will be sent to a potential employer via e-mail, posted on a career-related web site, such as the Monster Board (www.monster.com), or included within

☆ ☆ **WARNING** ☆ ☆

There is no room for false information on your resume or in your cover letters. Most employers will check all past employment, references, and other information you provide. Some employers even conduct full background checks on applicants. If it's discovered that you've lied or stretched the truth, you will not get hired.

TIP

If you're not confident writing your own resume you can hire a professional resume writer at a cost of $50 to $200. Use any internet search engine and the search phrase "resume writer" to find someone capable of creating or fine-tuning your resume. You will, however, be responsible for providing the writer with accurate information and details about yourself that will be incorporated into the resume.

an online resume database. Many employers accept electronic resumes via their web sites, but have a predefined resume form that must be completed online. This also holds true for the majority of career-related web sites.

When creating an electronic resume, adhere exactly to the formatting specifications provided by the employer or career-related web site. This means offering only the information requested in each field of an online form. You'll discover that the information being requested is exactly the same as what would be incorporated into a traditional, printed, chronological resume; it's just the formatting that is different.

One difference between an electronic format and a traditional (printed) format is that as you're writing the electronic resume, you'll want to use keywords, as opposed to action words or descriptive phrases, to present your employment history, skills, and education. An electronic resume can be used for three main purposes:

1. To find and apply for jobs online using popular career-related web sites, such as the Monster Board (www.monster.com), HotJobs (http://hotjobs.yahoo.com), and CareerBuilder (www.careerbuilder.com).
2. To apply for and submit your resume directly to an employer by visiting the company's web site or sending your resume directly via e-mail. When you do this, your resume and electronic cover letter can be incorporated into the body of an e-mail or sent as an attachment to your e-mail.
3. To add your resume to one of many online resume databases that are used as applicant search tools by potential employers, headhunters, and employment agencies.

While you will not have to deal with issues such as choosing the right paper, picking the perfect font, or formatting your resume to look perfect on the printed page, there are other issues you will need to contend with when creating an electronic resume.

When completing an online resume form, be sure you fill in all fields with the appropriate information only. Never attempt to be clever or creative by trying to add information that isn't requested in a specific field in order to include extra information about yourself. Be mindful of limitations for each field. For example, a field that allows for a job description to be entered may have space for a maximum of only 50 words,

TIP

There are no standard guidelines to follow when creating an electronic resume, because employers use different computer systems and software. Thus, it is important that you adhere to the individual requirements of each employer in terms of formatting, saving, and sending your resume electronically.

so the description you enter needs to provide all of the relevant information (using keywords), but also be written concisely. Since an electronic resume is as important as a traditional one, consider printing out the online form first and then spending time thinking about how you will fill in each field (or answer each question). You can also refer to information already included within your traditional printed resumes.

When sending a resume via e-mail, begin the message as you would a cover letter with the same information. You can then either attach the resume file to the e-mail message or paste the resume text within the message (but make sure the formatting remains intact).

Always be sure to include your e-mail address as well as your regular mailing address and phone number(s) within all e-mail correspondence. Never assume an employer will receive your message and simply hit "respond" or "reply" using their e-mail software to contact you.

Creating an Electronic Resume

It's usually easier to first create a traditional (printed) resume and then edit it accordingly to fit into an electronic format. The following tips will help you create and properly format your electronic resume:

- Avoid using bullets or other symbols. Instead of a bullet, use an asterisk (*) or a dash (-). Instead of using the percentage sign (%), for example, spell out the word "percent." (In your resume, write 15 percent, not 15%.)
- Use the spell check feature of the software used to create your electronic resume and then proofread the document carefully. Just as applicant tracking software used by employers is designed to pick out keywords from your resume that showcase you as a qualified applicant, such software can also instantly count the number of typos and spelling errors in your document and report that to an employer.
- Avoid using multiple columns, tables, or charts within your resume document.
- Within the text, avoid abbreviations—spell everything out. For example, use the word "director" instead of "dir." or "vice president" as opposed to "VP." For degrees, however, it is acceptable to use terms such as "MBA," "BA," and "Ph.D."

Keywords are the backbone of any good electronic resume. If you don't incorporate keywords, your resume will not be properly processed by the employer's applicant tracking software.

Choosing the right keywords to incorporate into your resume is a skill that takes some creativity and plenty of thought.

For example, each job title, job description, skill, degree, license, or other piece of information you list within your resume should be descriptive, self-explanatory, and among the keywords the potential employer's applicant tracking software is on the lookout for as it evaluates your resume. One excellent resource that can help you select the best keywords to use within your electronic resume is the *Occupational Outlook Handbook* published by the U.S. Department of Labor (http://stats.bls.gov/oco/home.htm).

Using Resume Creation Software

While you can download free resume templates for use with Microsoft Word to format a resume (http://office.microsoft.com/en-us/templates/), using specialized resume creation software takes much of the hassle out of the process. In addition to handling the formatting of your resume, specialized resume software will also recommend proper phrasing, check for spelling and grammatical errors, and help you organize your information so it fits neatly on a single page.

WinWay Resume Deluxe ($39.95, WinWay Corporation, www.winway.com), is a full-featured, yet easy-to-use resume and cover letter creation tool that also offers a wide range of tools ideal for job seekers. This software will walk you through the resume creation process and prompt you for the required information by asking a series of questions about your desired position, experience, and education. The Resume Wizard built into this software contains a database of more than 13,000 resume examples that can be customized to suit any profession or job title. The software will also format your resume to be printed, allow you to create a PDF file, or create an electronic format for easy e-mailing.

One nice feature of the WinWay Resume Deluxe software is that when it comes to describing your employment history, education, and experience, you can tap into a database of more than 100,000 powerful and descriptive phrases, then use the software's Resume Auditor feature to catch any mistakes that go beyond just spelling and punctuation. For example, if the software notices you earned a degree more than 20 years ago, this is an indication of your age (which you might not want to provide within your resume). The software will recommend alternate ways to convey relevant information without revealing details that could keep you from being considered for your desired position.

Other tools built into WinWay Resume Deluxe allow you to create and format matching cover letters and printed envelopes using a variety of fonts, layouts, and designs. Best of all, this software is template-driven, meaning that from a design and formatting standpoint, all of the work is done for you, once you select the template you wish to use. WinWay Resume Deluxe can be purchased directly from the company's web site or wherever software is sold.

Resume Maker Premier from Individual Software ($39.95, www.individualsoftware.com) is another specialized resume creation software package that will help you create, format, and distribute professional-looking resumes and cover letters, and find jobs to apply for. The resume creation module of the software offers "1-Click Styles" for quickly formatting your resume, and a database of more than 13,000 career-specific resume samples. As you're writing your resume, you can tap into a list of more than 150,000 prewritten phrases to add power to your resume, and choose from a wide range of fonts. With a few additional clicks of the mouse, you can then post your resume on more than 100 career-related web sites.

Writing Powerful Cover Letters

If you already understand the format of a typical business letter and know what you are trying to convey within your cover letter, creating this document is relatively easy. Whether you are creating a cover letter that will be printed out and then hand-delivered, mailed, or faxed (as opposed to e-mailed with

TIP

Individual Software offers two less expensive versions of Resume Maker Premier, which start at $19.95, but offer fewer features. These software packages are available from office supply superstores, wherever computer software is sold, or via the company's web site.

TIP

Your cover letter and resume should summarize your accomplishments, education, and skills using plain English. These documents must incorporate perfect spelling and grammar and be written in a formal business style.

an electronic resume), the content and format of the cover letter are the same.

As a general rule, never submit your resume to a potential employer unless it is accompanied by a personalized and custom-written cover letter. This is an important companion document to your resume. A cover letter serves as your initial introduction to a potential employer. It should get the recipient interested in reading your resume.

Just as your resume should be one, 8.5-by-11-inch page in length, your cover letter should also be kept to less than one page. The shorter the better, since most people do not have time to read long letters.

A cover letter is designed to accompany your resume. Create these documents with synergy in mind when it comes to appearance and content. If you are creating a printed resume and cover letter (as opposed to an electronic resume for use with the internet), always use the same paper, fonts, and typestyles for both documents. Virtually all employers put great value on an applicant with strong written and verbal communication skills. A resume is typically a series of bulleted lists and short sentences, but a cover letter represents an actual writing sample that will be evaluated.

The Purpose of a Cover Letter

Your cover letter should not duplicate too much information that is already in your resume. Instead, you want to use a cover letter to do the following:

- Introduce yourself
- State exactly what job or position you are applying for
- Seize the attention of the reader
- Pique the reader's interest
- Convey information about yourself that is not in your resume
- Briefly demonstrate your skills and accomplishments

> ☆ ☆ **WARNING** ☆ ☆
>
> Unless you impress an employer with your cover letter first, many human resources professionals will not bother to read your resume. Thus, there is a chance your cover letter will be your only opportunity to convince a potential employer you are a viable job candidate. Both the wording and the overall appearance of your cover letter should complement your resume.

- Convince the reader to review your resume
- Ask the reader for an action to be taken (such as inviting you to come in for an interview)

If you want your cover letter and resume to stand out, they need to look extremely professional, as if you have put considerable thought and attention into the appearance of these documents. First impressions, in this case, are extremely important.

While the reader of your cover letter will, of course, be looking at the letter's content and meaning, your writing style, spelling, punctuation, and the choice format for the document will all be evaluated. What you say in your cover letter is important, but you should also think carefully about how you want to say it, and make sure that your overall presentation is professional and visually appealing. Each cover letter should be custom written for the job you are applying for, and be personalized using the name and title of the recipient.

Creating and Personalizing Your Cover Letters

Before sending your cover letter and resume to anyone, call the recipient's office and ask for their full name and title. Obtain the correct spelling of both the recipient's and the company's names.

It is also critical to confirm the recipient's gender, so you can address the envelope and cover letter to Mr., Ms., or Mrs. (insert last name). Refrain from making assumptions.

Before sitting down to write your cover letter, obtain the following information and make sure it's accurate:

- The recipient's full name
- The recipient's job title
- The company name
- The recipient's mailing address
- The recipient's phone number
- The title of the position you're applying for
- The recipient's fax number (optional)
- The recipient's e-mail address (optional)

In terms of the letter's format, at the top, be sure to list your full name, address, phone number(s), and e-mail address. If you have personalized stationary that matches your resume paper, use it. Your contact information should be followed by the recipient's address and the date (using a standard business letter format).

Next add the salutation. This is much like saying "hello" in a verbal conversation and should be something such as

- Dear (insert recipient's first name):
- Dear Mr./Mrs./Ms./Dr. (insert recipient's last name):

Next comes the opening paragraph of your letter. Keep it short and simple. This paragraph should show who you are and why you are writing the letter. Keep this part of your cover letter to two or three sentences. Be sure to mention what job or position you are applying for, especially if you are responding to an ad.

Following the opening paragraph, use the next paragraph or two within the body of your letter to set yourself apart from the competition. Make sure you convey reasons why you are the best applicant for the job you're applying for. Addressing the employer's needs is the primary goal for this portion of the cover letter.

By conducting research about the potential employer (and by reviewing the wording of the ad or job description you're responding to), you should have a basic understanding of what the employer's needs are. In your cover letter, describe how you (with your education, skills, and experience) can meet those needs and help the company achieve its goals.

Use the next paragraph of your letter to answer this question: What is it about the employer that piqued your interest? This is your opportunity to kiss up, compliment the employer, and demonstrate you have done some research about the organization and industry.

The next section of your letter should be a request for the reader to take action, such as inviting you in for an interview. Finally, your letter should conclude with a formal closure and your signature. Be sure to thank the reader for their interest, time, and consideration.

Formatting Your Cover Letter

All correspondence with a potential employer, with the exception of a thank-you note, should be typed or created on a computer, not handwritten. Figure 8.2 is a sample showing how you should format your cover letter on a printed page.

FIGURE 8.2: SAMPLE COVER LETTER

Your Address
Your Phone Number
Your Fax Number (Optional)
Your E-Mail Address (Optional)

Date

Recipient's Full Name
Recipient's Title
Company Name
Address
City, State, Zip Code

Dear (Mr./Mrs./Mrs./Dr.) (Insert Recipient's Last Name):

Opening Paragraph

Support Paragraph #1

Support Paragraph #2

Request for Action Paragraph

Closing Paragraph

Sincerely,
(Your Signature)
(Your Full Name Typed)

Writing Thank-You Notes

While your cover letter and resume should be typed, it's appropriate to send a handwritten thank-you note immediately after participating in a job interview. You can buy nice thank-you note cards at any stationery or office supply store. Keep the note short and to the point, but be sure to include something that references what you discussed with the interviewer, so you can remind the recipient of who you are.

Figure 8.3 is a sample of what you might write within the thank-you note:

FIGURE 8.3: SAMPLE THANK-YOU NOTE

Dear Mr. Smith,

Thank you for taking the time to interview me for the salesperson position at The ABC Company. I am very excited about this opportunity. Given the company's need for a more energetic and experienced sales force, I hope you agree that my qualifications and experience make me the ideal candidate for the job.

Should you have any more questions, please call me anytime at (555) 555-5555, or drop me an e-mail at johnsmith@e-mailaddress.com. I look forward to the possibility of working for The ABC Company in the near future.

Sincerely,
John Smith

Next, the Interview

Creating a powerful resume that properly showcases essential information about you as an applicant is important. If your resume and cover letter do their jobs properly, you should be invited to participate in a job interview. This is your chance to sell yourself as the ideal applicant for the job—both on the telephone and in person. The next chapter focuses on how to master interview techniques that will help you land the job you want.

CHAPTER 9

Job Interview **Techniques**

WHAT'S IN THIS CHAPTER

- Preparing for a job interview
- How to answer interview questions
- Sample interview questions
- Questions for you to ask
- Negotiating your salary and compensation package

Creating a well-written resume and cover letter will help you get noticed by potential employers. It will be how well you perform during your interviews, however, that will determine whether you get hired for a job you're qualified to fill. Once you've pinpointed what you believe to be the perfect job opportunity for you—one you're convinced you'd prosper in and enjoy—you'll still need to convince the employer.

A job interview is an opportunity for you to prove that you are more qualified to fill a job opening than any other applicants applying for that same position. While all of the applicants may meet the core education requirements for the job, for example, each applicant offers a unique skill set and combination of past work experiences. Your main responsibility during an interview is to establish your credentials, and then focus on what's unique about you that will allow you to exceed the expectations of the employer if you're offered the position.

How well you promote yourself during the interview will be a primary factor in whether or not you're offered a job. It will also help determine how much you'll be paid if offered the job. While most employers have predetermined salary ranges for each position, there is often some leeway. By successfully promoting yourself and your personality, skills, experience, education, and overall potential during the interview process, you're more apt to be able to negotiate the best possible salary and compensation package for yourself.

This chapter focuses on how to handle each job interview situation in order to position yourself as a highly marketable and valuable applicant—as well as the ideal candidate for the position you're applying for.

Preparing for a Job Interview

Assuming you've applied for jobs that you're qualified to fill, your phone should begin ringing once you've submitted your resume, cover letter, and perhaps an employment application for each of those positions. The hope is that you'll be invited to participate in in-person interviews with potential employers. As soon as you answer the phone, be sure to act professionally, while allowing your friendly and outgoing personality to come through. Write down the person's name, phone number, company, and address, as well as the date and time you set for the interview. Before setting an interview appointment, check your schedule to make sure the date and time you choose work. You never want to have to reschedule a job interview due to a conflict.

Once you've set a day and time for your interview, confirm where the interview will take place (get the exact address, including the floor number and office number), as well as the name and title of the person you'll be meeting with. If necessary, obtain driving directions to where the meeting will be held, or get the address so you can use an online service, such as MapQuest (www.mapquest.com) or Yahoo! Maps (http://maps.yahoo.com), to get detailed directions. After confirming all of the information, thank the person for their call.

TIP

When scheduling a job interview, try to give yourself 24 to 48 hours of lead time so that you can conduct proper research, prepare for the interview, and decide what to wear.

Now that you have a job interview scheduled, the first step in preparing for that interview is to do your research. Never go into a job interview unprepared. Make sure the research materials you use are up-to-date and accurate.

Before applying for a job, you should have already done some basic research about the position and the company. Now that you've been invited for an interview, you'll want to conduct more extensive research about the job you're looking to fill and about the employer. One of the best resources available to you to conduct this research is the company's web site. If applicable, also obtain a copy of the company's annual report (if it's a publicly traded company). From services like PR Newswire (www.prnewswire.com), you may also be able to obtain copies of press releases issued by the company. The internet can also be used to track down recent articles about the company that have appeared in newspapers and magazines.

In addition to learning as much as you can about the company and the person you'll be interviewing with, conduct research about the industry as a whole. Learn who the major

TIP

To find any company's web site using a search engine such as Yahoo! or Google, simply enter the company's name as your search phrase. To find information about Fortune 500 companies, visit http://money.cnn.com/magazines/fortune/fortune500/.

competitors are, what the state of the industry is, and what challenges the industry as a whole is facing. Consider reading at least three recent issues of trade publications that cater to the industry you want to work in. Reading recent issues of *The Wall Street Journal, Business Week, The New York Times, Forbes,* and *Investor's Business Daily,* for example, can help get you up to speed on industry trends, as well as other more general business-related information. The business section of your local newspaper can also be an informative resource.

Prepare a list of intelligent questions you'd like to ask the employer. Also, anticipate what questions you'll be asked and rehearse how you'll answer them in a way that showcases your personality, verbal communication skills, intelligence, and overall qualifications.

The next step in interview preparation involves deciding what you'll wear to the interview. Choose an outfit that's formal and appropriate for the position you're looking to fill. Make sure the outfit is compatible with the company's dress code and corporate culture. As you select your outfit, dress to impress, but avoid any clothing or accessories that stand out, that might attract negative attention, or that could be distracting to the interviewer. For example, wearing a lot of flashy jewelry or an overly bright colored tie might distract the interviewer and detract from the professional image you're trying to convey.

How to Answer Interview Questions

As part of your job interview preparation, determine the types of questions the interviewer will most likely ask you. Once you begin participating in multiple interviews, you'll learn that you are often asked similar questions over and over again. Spend time developing well-thought-out, complete, and intelligent answers to common questions.

Here are some tips for answering all of the interviewer's questions:

- Avoid talking down to an interviewer or making them feel less intelligent than you are.
- Be prepared to answer the same questions multiple times. Make sure your answers are consistent. Never reply, "You already asked me that."
- Don't be evasive, especially if you're asked about negative aspects of your employment history.
- Don't lie or stretch the truth.
- Never apologize for negative information regarding your past.

- Never imply that a question is "stupid."
- Use complete sentences and proper English.
- As you answer each question, refrain from disclosing too much personal information that could be held against you. For example, don't say that you have young children or are planning to have children in the near future. An employer might think that you'll miss too much work in order to deal with child-related emergencies.
- Avoid discussing topics that relate to your marital status, sexual orientation, age, religion, or political affiliations. Also, avoid any controversial topics.
- It's OK to take a moment to collect your thoughts before responding to a question. If necessary, you can refer to your research or notes to obtain specific pieces of information.
- Always allow the interviewer to finish asking their question before you respond.
- Maintain a professional attitude throughout the interview. Never become overly emotional. Remember, a job interview is a chance to show off your professionalism and personality. Refrain from making off-color jokes or comments.
- During each interview, focus on information about yourself that your employer would be interested in, but that isn't necessarily included in your resume. Feel free to discuss relevant past work experiences, how you've

used specific skills, or how you could use your training and education to excel in the job if you're hired.

- Be polite and professional with everyone you meet when visiting a company for an interview including secretaries, receptionists, and anyone else you're introduced to.

Sample Interview Questions

Now that you understand the best way to answer whatever questions are posed to you, here's a list of common questions that interviewers often choose to ask. Practice answering these questions as completely and succinctly as possible. Rehearse your responses, and be sure to control your facial expressions and body language while you're answering each question.

- What can you tell me about yourself that isn't listed in your resume?
- Why have you decided to pursue this career path and this particular job opening?
- Why do you believe you're the best applicant for the job?
- What do you think sets you apart from other applicants?
- Why are you leaving (or why did you leave) your most recent job?
- What was your greatest accomplishment at your last job?
- Thus far in your career, what has been your biggest failure? What did you learn from the experience? How did you overcome it?
- What are your long-term goals?

☆ ☆ WARNING ☆ ☆

There are specific questions your employer is not allowed to ask you. These questions include: Are you a U.S. citizen? Where were you or your parents born? What is your native tongue? What is your religion? How old are you? What year did you graduate from high school or college? What is your sexual orientation? Are you married? Do you have children? Do you plan to have children in the near future? What are your child-care arrangements? Do you have any illnesses? Be sure to avoid answering these questions or more open-ended questions designed to probe for highly personal information that you do not want taken into consideration when a potential employer is making their hiring decision.

- What have you heard about this company? Why does working here appeal to you?
- If hired, what do you think you'll be able to contribute to help this company achieve its goals?
- What are your biggest professional strengths?
- What can you tell me about your personal situation?
- How does your previous work experience relate to the job you're applying for here?
- What type of salary and benefits package are you looking for?

- What specific skills do you possess that will help you excel in the job you're applying for?
- What, if anything, would keep you from meeting the responsibilities of this job if you were hired?
- How flexible are you in terms of your work schedule? Are you able and willing to work overtime, nights, weekends, or holidays?

Questions for You to Ask

One of your goals during a job interview should be to engage in a two-way conversation. Don't just answer a question and wait for the next one. It's appropriate for you, as the applicant, to ask intelligent and relevant questions. The following are sample questions you might want to ask during the interview. It's OK to write out these questions and refer to them during your interview.

- Could you provide me with a more detailed job description or a list of the primary responsibilities related to the position I'm applying for?
- If I get hired for this job, what would your expectations for me be within the first three months, six months, and one year?
- Why is the position I'm applying for currently available? Is the division I'll be working in expanding?
- How would you describe the overall corporate culture at this company?
- What management style is used to run the business?

- What can you tell me about my potential supervisors or superiors?
- Does the job I'm applying for require a lot of travel? If so, how much and to where?
- Could you describe what my typical work day would be like if I were hired?
- Would my work schedule be flexible, or would I be required to work specific hours, such as 9:00 A.M. to 5:00 P.M., Monday through Friday?
- How do you evaluate your employees and how often are performance reviews done?
- What type of on-the-job training is available?
- If I were interested in advancing my career while working for this company, what opportunities would be available to me in the future? Within what time period?
- What challenges is your company facing? What plans are in place to overcome these challenges?
- In the past few years, how as the company evolved? Has it grown or downsized?

Job Interview Dos and Don'ts

A job interview is your opportunity to sell yourself to a potential employer by demonstrating through your words, appearance, attitude, and body language that you're the very best candidate to fill a particular job opening. Hiring decisions are made as a result of how you conduct yourself during interviews.

An employer's decision about whether or not to hire you will be based on your skills, experience, and educational background, and how well you represent yourself and perform during your job interview.

The following strategies will help you to properly prepare for an interview and make a positive first impression:

- Before the interview, do research about the company you're interviewing with and the industry you'll be working in, and try to learn as much as possible about the individual who will be conducting the interview.
- As part of your preparation, participate in a mock interview with a friend, relative, or career counselor. Practice answering common interview questions out loud, and compile a list of at least five intelligent questions you can ask the employer during the interview.
- Be sure to get a good night's sleep before the interview. You want to look and feel rested.
- Before your interview, take a shower, shampoo your hair, clean your fingernails, brush your teeth, shave, and apply antiperspirant. Your appearance is the first thing a potential employer is going to notice when you arrive for an interview.
- Make sure what you'll be wearing to your interview is clean and wrinkle-free and that it fits perfectly. Also, be sure your shoes are shined and coordinated with your outfit.
- Before arriving for the interview, make several extra copies of your resume, letters of recommendation, and

list of references. Have these documents with you at the interview. You'll also want to bring your daily planner, along with your research materials, a pad, and a pen. All of this paperwork will fit nicely in a briefcase or portfolio.

- The morning of your interview, read a local newspaper or watch a morning news program. You'll want to be aware of the day's news events and be able to discuss them with the interviewer. Many interviewers like to start off an interview with general chit-chat. Your goal is to appear knowledgeable about what's happening in the world around you.
- Arrive for your interview at least 15 minutes early and check in with the receptionist. While it's OK for an interviewer to keep you, the applicant, waiting, it's never acceptable for the applicant to show up for an interview even one minute late. Next to being unprepared for the interview, arriving late is the worst mistake you can make.
- From the moment you arrive at the interview location, act professionally. Be polite to everyone, including secretaries and receptionists.
- As the interview gets under way, sit up straight. Listen carefully to the questions posed to you and take a moment to think about each answer. Respond using complete sentences. Words such as *yeah, nope,* and *umm* should not be used as part of your professional vocabulary.

- Throughout the entire interview, in addition to what you say, you will be evaluated based on your conduct and body language. Control your nervous habits. If you know what these habits are, they'll be easier to control in stressful situations.
- During the later part of your interview, make a point to come right out and ask for the job you're applying for. Explain exactly why you want the job, what you can offer the company, and why you're the best candidate to fill the position.

At the conclusion of the interview, thank the interviewer for their time, and determine whether any follow-up is required on your part. Do you need to provide additional materials? Also, find out what the next step is. When will you hear back from the potential employer?

TIP

Within 24 hours after each job interview, mail a handwritten and personalized thank-you note to the person or people who interviewed you. Thank them for their time and interest. Mention how much you'd enjoy working at the company if given the opportunity. In one or two sentences, summarize once again what you can offer that sets you apart from the other applicants.

Negotiating Your Salary and Compensation Package

Refrain from discussing salary and benefits until after you've been offered a job, unless the topic is brought up by the interviewer. When the topic does come up, be prepared to discuss salary and benefits intelligently. Make sure you've done your research so you know what a typical salary is for someone in this position with your experience and qualifications, within your geographic area, and within your industry. Also, have a realistic salary in mind that you'd like to receive, and know what salary you absolutely need in order to maintain (or slightly improve) your current quality of life and cover your living expenses.

Consider the salary and benefits portion of the negotiation process to be separate. Focus first on the salary and then on negotiating the best overall benefits package, based on what you want and need. Remember, every benefit and perk that's offered has a cash value associated with it.

When engaged in a salary negotiation, focus on creating a win-win situation, maintaining a calm and professional demeanor, and remembering your goals. One of the most important skills you can use when negotiating is your ability to listen. Your creativity can also be useful, especially when negotiating benefits and perks. While you might not be able to get your potential employer to boost a salary offer, you might be able to negotiate for perks and benefits that have a significant financial value. For example, you'll often find it easier to negotiate for more paid vacation days, additional paid sick days (personal days), a larger expense account, a better employee discount, or more health and life insurance coverage than for a higher base salary.

The next chapter focuses on better understanding benefits and perks.

☆ ☆ WARNING ☆ ☆

Use the job interview as an opportunity to learn as much about the position as possible to ensure that it hasn't been misrepresented. Make sure the job you think you're accepting is really what's being offered. The best way to do this is to ask plenty of questions about the position, job-related responsibilities, and employer's expectations.

CHAPTER 10

Every Benefit Has **a Cash Value**

WHAT'S IN THIS CHAPTER

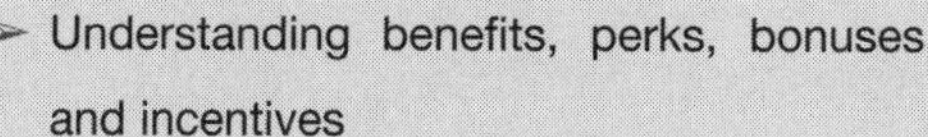

- Understanding benefits, perks, bonuses, and incentives
- Deciding what you want and need
- A raise or promotion could be in your future!

Benefits and perks are forms of compensation that go beyond your base salary or hourly wage, but provide extra reasons and financial incentives to work for a specific employer. Every benefit and perk offered has a dollar value associated with it, because your employer is picking up some or all of the cost of what's being offered.

Benefits and perks are designed to improve your quality of life and make your job more enjoyable. This chapter focuses on what benefits and perks may be offered by a potential employer, and will help you determine what you actually want and need.

The time to consider perks and benefits being offered by an employer is after you receive a firm job offer. That's the time to negotiate your salary and overall compensation package, which includes perks and benefits. A job offer often has many components, which should be considered separately to determine if you want take the position being offered.

Some of the things that comprise a job offer and that you'll want to consider before accepting it include

- base salary;
- commissions (if applicable);
- future earnings and upward mobility potential;
- incentives and bonuses;
- medical insurance and other benefits;
- paid holidays, sick days, and vacation days;
- perks offered;

- possible bonuses and incentives;
- potential overtime pay;
- prenegotiated severance package;
- relocation benefits (if applicable);
- requirements of the job (primary responsibilities);
- retirement plan;
- sign-on bonuses;
- stock participation and profit sharing;
- the ability of the job to help you achieve your long-term career-related goals;
- the corporate culture and environment where you'll be working;
- the employer and their reputation;
- the employer's expectations;
- the impact accepting the job will have on you and your family;
- training and education opportunities (such as tuition reimbursement); and
- your co-workers and superiors and whether or not you'll get along with them.

While you'll definitely want to concern yourself with how much you'll be paid and what your *take-home pay* (after taxes and other deductions) will be, focus on the overall compensation package being offered, including all of the benefits and perks. Every employer offers a different assortment of benefits and perks. What's offered to you and when it's offered will be determined by the position you'll be filling.

Take-home pay. This is the amount of money from your paycheck that actually goes into your pocket. It represents your base salary, minus deductions, costs, and expenses taken out automatically by your employer for income taxes, mandatory expenses such as Social Security, and unemployment, and your contribution toward benefits.

Once you receive a job offer that's accompanied by a salary and overall compensation package, it's essential to ensure that your take-home pay will actually cover all of your living expenses and allow you to maintain or improve your quality of life. Your take-home pay is your base salary *minus* all of the taxes and other expenses and benefit contributions deducted by the employer and the government. Use the following formula to help calculate your actual take-home pay:

Base salary:	**$______**
Costs/expenses automatically deducted from your paycheck:	
State and local income taxes (if applicable):	- $______
Federal income taxes:	- $______
Social Security/Medicare:	- $______
Other mandatory deductions (unemployment, etc.):	- $______
Total employee contributions toward benefits:	- $______
Take-home pay:	**$______**

While some employers pick up the full cost of benefits, in many situations, each employee is required to make a financial contribution to the benefits they want to receive (in essence sharing the cost with their employer). Depending on your job title and your employer, you'll often be able to pick and choose which benefits you want. All applicable contributions will automatically be deducted from your paycheck by your employer. Popular benefits that might require you to make a regular financial contribution include the following:

- Child care
- Dental insurance for you and your family
- Dependent care assistance program
- Health insurance for you and your family
- Life insurance
- Long-term disability insurance
- Retirement or pension plan—401(k)
- Short-term disability insurance
- Stock participation plan

Understanding Benefits, Perks, Bonuses, and Incentives

In addition to the popular benefits offered by many employers to full-time employees—such as health insurance, paid sick days, and paid vacation days—a wide range of *perks* might also be offered. A perk is an extra expense that your employer picks up that somehow improves your work experience or quality of life. Popular job-related perks include

- casual Fridays or half-day Fridays;
- child care;
- employee discounts on products and services;

- paid commuting expenses (gas, tolls, parking, mileage reimbursement, etc.);
- flexible scheduling;
- free coffee, sodas, and snacks;
- free or subsidized lunches or an employee cafeteria meal plan;
- health club membership;
- low interest loans; and
- use of a company car (leased by your employer).

If you were to pay for these expenses out of pocket, using after-tax dollars, they'd add up quickly. If your employer pays these expenses on your behalf, however, this represents money you save. Unlimited free coffee while at work, for example, could save you $10 or more per day. This represents a savings of several hundred dollars per month. If you receive use of a company car as a perk, you may not have to purchase or lease a car and make a monthly payment of several hundred dollars. Company cars tend to be given to people filling sales or field representative jobs that require a lot of travel, and to those in middle-management and executive-level positions.

Benefit. This represents a form of nonwage compensation offered to an employee. A benefit can fall into one of the following categories: paid leave (vacations, holidays, sick leave); supplementary pay (overtime pay and extra pay for work on holidays and weekends); retirement; insurance (life insurance, health benefits, short-term disability, and/or long-term disability insurance); and all legally required benefits (including Social

Security and Medicare, federal and state unemployment insurance taxes, and workers' compensation).

Make sure you understand each benefit being offered and what's included. For example, on a holiday you may not have to work, but you may not get paid either. If you're offered vacation time, you want to know if these are paid or unpaid vacation days, how many vacation days you're entitled to per year, and what limitations or restrictions are placed on when you can take those vacation days. Even if you're entitled to two weeks' worth of vacation time, some employers may restrict you from taking more than five to seven vacation days in a row. You might also have to block off or reserve your vacation periods weeks or months in advance. If you have children who are following a strict school-related schedule, having vacation days that don't correspond with that schedule could impact your ability to plan family vacations.

Perk. A perk is a small benefit that improves your work experience or quality of life, such as paid parking, free coffee, employee discounts on products or services, subsidized lunches, health club membership, or use of a company car. Perks are expenses you'd otherwise incur yourself that your employer pays for.

Bonus / incentive. This is a cash payment (in addition to base salary) that's made to employees who achieve a predefined goal or objective. Some employers also offer a one-time holiday bonus to employees as a reward for a profitable year.

Deciding What You Want and Need

There are some benefits such as health insurance that you'll definitely want to take advantage of if they're offered by your employer. Other benefits may be offered, but may or may not be of interest to you, based on your personal and financial situation. If you're single with no children, working for an employer that offers free child care won't be beneficial to you. When evaluating a job offer, figure out which benefits are offered by your employer that are automatically included in your compensation package, and which benefits are optional, but ones you might want to take advantage of.

Next, figure out whether the cost of each benefit is being entirely paid for by your employer, or you'll be required to make a financial contribution. Also, you'll want to determine what each benefit includes. There are many types and levels of health

TIP

Fortune magazine annually publishes a list of the 100 best companies to work for. To access this list, point your web browser to http://money.cnn.com/magazines/fortune/bestcompanies/2006/full_list/. The *Working Mother* web site (www.workingmother.com) offers an annual list of the most family-friendly companies to work for. Use research like this to help you pursue the best job opportunities.

insurance, for example. What coverage is being offered and how much of a co-pay will you be responsible for when making doctors' appointments, paying for prescription medications, or visiting the hospital on an emergency basis? In terms of life insurance, is a term-life or whole-life policy being offered? How much insurance coverage is included? Is it a $10,000, $100,000, or $1,000,000 life insurance policy, for example?

When reviewing each benefit, think about your need, the level of coverage or the amount of the benefit, and the cost to you to acquire the benefit through your employer versus obtaining the same thing independently as an out-of-pocket, after-tax, personal expense.

After a job offer is made, someone from the company's human resources department should be willing to sit down with you to review all of the benefits and perks being offered. Understand that every single benefit or perk has a dollar value attached to it. Figure out how much money you'll ultimately be saving (from your take-home pay), based on the benefits and perks being covered by your employer. The total value of the perks and benefits being offered should be considered part of your overall compensation package when determining whether an offer is attractive. A lower base salary with a more comprehensive benefits package, for example, may be more financially viable for you. Crunch the numbers for yourself so you can understand exactly what's being offered.

For middle-management or executive-level jobs, understanding the compensation package being offered is often a bit confusing. The best thing you can do is focus on your needs,

☆ ☆ WARNING ☆ ☆

Based on the job you're accepting and the number of hours per week you'll be working, you might not be eligible for certain benefits and perks. For example, many employers offer health insurance only to full-time employees—not to part-time workers, interns, or temps.

and then read all of the benefit-related materials provided by your company (or the third-party benefit provider). Also, consider sitting down with your accountant to help you review each job offer from a financial standpoint to ensure you'll be able to cover all of your living expenses and that you fully understand all of the benefits you'll be receiving.

TIP

Before accepting a compensation package, which includes perks and benefits, determine exactly when these benefits and perks will be available to you. Some employers don't offer health insurance benefits, for example, until after an employee has been on the job for 90 days. Others offer benefits after 30 days or as soon as someone is hired. When you become eligible for benefits can sometimes be negotiated.

TIP

One way some people choose to improve their incomes (over time) is to quit their jobs and open their own businesses. Even with all of the right resources at your disposal, this too can be a risky endeavor. Operating your own business and becoming self-employed can provide an incredible opportunity for some people, but it requires a tremendous time and financial commitment. One way to reduce the risk associated with starting your own business and becoming your own boss is to pursue some type of legitimate franchise opportunity.

The Unofficial Guide to Opening a Franchise ($18.99, Wiley Publishing) offers an easy-to-understand and comprehensive overview of how to become a successful franchisee. On the internet, the Entrepreneur Franchise Zone (www.entrepreneur.com/franchises/index.html) is an extremely informative and free resource for prospective franchisees interested in learning about the thousands of franchise opportunities available.

Make sure that whatever insurance coverage you're getting, for example, doesn't overlap with coverage your spouse's benefits package provides, or with coverage you're already paying for separately. If you'll be changing insurance companies or providers for your health or life insurance, for example, make sure there will be no lapses in coverage and that the extent of your new coverage will be as good, if not better than, your previous coverage.

A Raise or Promotion Could Be in Your Future!

By reading this book you have no doubt figured out that by working hard and proving your worth to an employer, you should be able to earn the salary you want and deserve, and avoid being underpaid. As you make important decisions relating to your career, always focus on the short and long term and on how the choices you make and the actions you take will impact your ability to achieve your goals.

Throughout your career, focus on constantly building your skill set, gaining new and valuable experiences, and demonstrating your worth to your employer. When it comes time to ask for a raise or promotion, adopt a well-thought-out and organized approach, using the tips and strategies featured throughout this book. While there is no substitute for hard work, it's essential that the work you do be noticed and appreciated by your employer.

Remember, if your goal is to attain a high-level position, but you're starting your career in an entry-level job, you have your work cut out for you. Be patient and persistent. Stay focused on your dreams and goals.

☆ ☆ WARNING ☆ ☆

Some people who are interested in earning more money opt to get involved with "get rich quick" schemes or "business opportunities" in order to increase their income without having to put in too much effort. Many of these so-called opportunities are pyramid schemes or multilevel marketing opportunities that rarely, if ever, live up to the promises made. If you want to earn more money, be prepared to work for it. There are no shortcuts. Avoid getting caught up in scams!

Glossary of **Raise-Related Terms**

The following is a summary of terminology used throughout this book. Understanding these terms can help you obtain the raise or promotion you want and deserve.

Base salary. This is the annual salary your employer pays you, before deductions are taken out and any commissions, bonuses, or incentives are added.

Benefit. This represents a form of nonwage compensation offered to an employee. A benefit can fall into one of the following categories: paid leave (vacations, holidays, sick leave); supplementary pay (overtime pay and extra pay for work on holidays and weekends); retirement; insurance (life insurance, health benefits, short-term disability, or long-term disability insurance); and all legally required benefits (including Social Security and Medicare, federal and state unemployment insurance taxes, and workers' compensation).

Bonus / incentive. This is a cash payment (in addition to base salary) that's made to employees who achieve a predefined goal or objective. Some employers also offer a one-time holiday bonus to employees as a reward for a profitable year.

Career path. Your career path is your roadmap for getting from the job you have now (or plan to get) to the dream job you want in the future. Each new job or position you take on throughout your career should move you one step closer to achieving your ultimate career goal(s). Ideally, you want to demonstrate a career path that has upward mobility, where you're earning more money, learning new skills, gaining additional experience, and taking on a higher level of responsibility with each new job or position you acquire.

Career-related goal. An objective you set for yourself that's career-related and that will somehow help you achieve more success in the future. A goal has a defined purpose, benefit, and deadline associated with it.

Chronological resume format. Using this widely accepted resume format, the applicant lists their employment history and education experience in reverse chronological order. This means your most recent jobs, for example, get listed first. This type of resume divides each category of information into sections, such as Objective, Employment History, Education, and Skills.

Dead-end job. This is a job or position that offers no possibility for advancement. The employer will not be willing to offer you a raise or promotion, regardless of your on-the-job performance, merit, or seniority with the company. The responsibilities you're given on the first day on the job will remain the same throughout your entire time holding that job or position. For most people, this is not the type of opportunity to pursue, because it really isn't an opportunity at all. it's simply a way to earn a paycheck. Most people who hold dead-end jobs wind up becoming frustrated or even hating their work.

Employee evaluation / performance review. Conducted by your superior at work, this is a periodic review of your on-the-job performance that becomes a permanent part of your personnel file. By combining an in-person meeting with a written report created by your superior, your employee evaluation is much like a school report card. It's often used as a tool to help employers determine whether employees are worthy of receiving a raise or promotion. If an employee's performance, attitude, and work are not measuring up, a negative evaluation can also be used to make the decision to fire, demote, or discipline an employee.

Job. A job is something you do to earn a paycheck that involves working part time or full time for an employer. In terms of this book, a job can be a stepping stone along a career path that you define for yourself, or it can be a way to pay your living expenses and bills that doesn't necessarily have anything to do with what you were trained to do or what you'd ultimately like to do for a life-long career.

Lateral promotion. This type of promotion offers new responsibilities and a different job title, but isn't accompanied by a pay raise, nor does it necessarily represent a step up the corporate ladder. It could simply mean a job change or transfer from one department, group, or division within your company to another.

Minimum wage. The federal government has set a minimum hourly wage that employers must pay nonexempt employees. Many states have set a minimum wage that's higher than what the federal government mandates. As of 2006, the federal minimum wage for covered, nonexempt employees was $5.15 per hour. At the time this book was written, legislation was in the works to increase the federal minimum wage to $7.25 starting sometime in 2007. In Massachusetts, for example, as of January 1, 2007, the minimum wage was $7.50 per hour. Effective January 1, 2008, the Massachusetts minimum wage will increase to $8 per hour. Across the country, the minimum wage for jobs that involve receiving tips is significantly lower. For a listing of each state's minimum wage, visit http://en.wikipedia.org/wiki/List_of_U.S._state_minimum_wages. If your income includes receiving tips, visit www.dol.gov/esa/programs/whd/state/tipped.htm to learn the state minimum wage for such a job.

New job promotion. Sometimes, to receive the recognition and compensation you deserve, it's necessary to change employers and pursue alternate opportunities. This type of promotion involves leaving your existing job and being hired by another employer to fill a more advanced position than your previous job. Your new job will come with a more impressive title, higher pay, and additional responsibilities. You'd qualify for this job based on your overall qualifications and past performance. You might pursue a new opportunity in order to achieve career advancement if your existing employer refuses to promote you when a promotion is deserved.

Perk. A perk is a small benefit that improves your work experience or quality of life, such as paid parking, free coffee, employee discounts on products or services, subsidized lunches, health club membership, or use of a company car. Perks are expenses you'd otherwise incur yourself that your employer pays for.

Personal skill set. This is your unique combination of skills that allows you to meet all of the responsibilities related to your job. Your skill set pertains to the collection of individual skills you have, and to your proficiency using each of those skills in the real world. Reading a book to enhance your public speaking skills, for example, will teach you the basics of that skill. You'll need to spend time practicing and fine-tuning the skill, however, before you become highly proficient using it on the job. Every job or position requires a different combination of skills. An employer's goal is to match up job requirements with people who have the proven skills necessary to meet the demands of each position.

Promotion. A promotion involves receiving a new job title, a new set of work-related responsibilities, a new set of expectations from your employer, and often a salary increase. A promotion can move you a step up the proverbial corporate ladder. Or, it can be a "lateral promotion," which means you're given a different set of responsibilities, but the same salary and compensation package, plus you maintain your current position in the overall corporate hierarchy where you work. Typically, employers reward employees who are dedicated, provide added value, exceed expectations in terms of performance, or achieve specific milestones. Employees must demonstrate their competence, qualifications, willingness, and ability to take on new responsibilities and provide greater value to an employer before they'll be considered for a promotion.

Qualifications. These are your unique combination of education, knowledge, work-related experience, skills, personality, mind-set, merit, and potential that makes you a suitable applicant to fill a specific job or position. Your qualifications will allow you to handle the requirements of a job, as well as meet or exceed an employer's expectations.

Raise. When your employer decides to pay you more money for continuing to work in the same job you already possess. Your responsibilities and job title won't necessarily change, but your salary or compensation package will improve. Some employers offer a raise to employees who remain on the job for a predetermined period of time. Others reward employees with raises for achieving specific milestones, accomplishments, or work-related goals. A raise is a preset amount of money that is reflected on an ongoing basis within your weekly, monthly, or annual paycheck. This is different from a one-time bonus or commission check, for example.

Standard promotion. This is when your existing employer gives you a new job title, more responsibilities, and a pay raise. You may also receive additional perks and benefits. The promotion represents a step up the corporate ladder, and typically means your employer will now have higher expectations for you in terms of performance.

Take-home pay. This is the amount of money from your paycheck that actually goes into your pocket. It represents your base salary, minus deductions, costs, and expenses taken out automatically by your employer for income taxes, mandatory expenses such as Social Security and unemployment, and your contribution toward benefits.

Index